Japanese
homestyle dishes

quick and delicious favorites

Your guide to preparing light and flavorful
Japanese meals at home—including classic Japanese recipes like
Healthy Miso Soup with Daikon, Nigiri Sushi with Shrimp,
Tuna and Eel, and Salmon Teriyaki.

PERIPLUS EDITIONS
Singapore • Hong Kong • Indonesia

Contents

MAIL ORDER SOURCES

Finding the ingredients for Asian home cooking has become very simple. Most supermarkets carry staples such as soy sauce, fresh ginger and lemongrass. Almost every large metropolitan area has Asian markets serving the local population—just check your local business directory. With the Internet, exotic Asian ingredients and cooking utensils can be easily found online. The following list is a good starting point of online merchants offering a wide variety of goods and services.

http://www.asiafoods.com
http://www.geocities.com/MadisonAvenue/8074/VarorE.html
http://dmoz.org/Shopping/Food/Ethnic_and_Regional/Asian/
http://templeofthai.com/
http://www.orientalpantry.com/
http://www.zestyfoods.com/
http://www.thaigrocer.com/Merchant/index.htm
http://asianwok.com/
http://pilipinomart.com/
http://www.indiangrocerynet.com/

The traditional Japanese meal is a work of art from the kitchen—balanced in color, texture and design. Applauded for its elegant simplicity and appreciated for its reliance on the freshest ingredients, the Japanese way of cooking fits easily into today's culinary scene, appealing to those who appreciate healthy eating, lighter portions and artistic presentations. At its best, a Japanese meal, with each course served on specially selected dinnerware, resembles a still life painting rendered in food and ceramics.

A Japanese meal can be put together quickly and easily. Most recipes call for only a handful of ingredients: rice, soy sauce, wasabi powder, sake, sesame seeds, dried shiitake mushrooms, ginger, wheat or buckwheat noodles, *dashi* stock, and tofu are some of the cornerstones of a Japanese meal. The trick is to keep a larder stocked with the Japanese essentials and to plan ahead—purchasing the fish, meat or vegetables the day they should be cooked.

The best known of all Japanese foods, sushi—tasty morsels of vinegared rice with slices of raw fish and a touch of wasabi underneath—has become so popular in the West that many restaurants now serve it as an appetizer. In large metropolitan areas, fresh sushi packs are even sold in well-stocked supermarkets. This volume includes easy-to-follow instructions for preparing various types of sushi, from the well known "finger" or Nigiri Sushi and California Rolls, to the hand-rolled "cone" or Temaki Sushi. Also presented are other Japanese all-time favorites such as Miso Soup, Traditional Seafood Sashimi Platter, Tempura and Grilled Skewered Chicken or *yakitori*.

All the recipes are light, healthy and delicious, and require no special skill or ingredients. This book promises a delightful venture into the world of Japanese cuisine.

Japanese Cooking Utensils

Bamboo rolling mat (*makisu*): Widely available from Asian supermarkets and very inexpensive, this simple bamboo mat is a must-have utensil for rolling rice inside wrappers of seaweed and for rolling Japanese omelets.

makisu

Fish-bone tweezers (*hone nuki*): A pair of flat-ended tweezers is always present in a Japanese kitchen for deboning fish.

Hotpot: A circular clay pot with a cover, used for cooking soups and stews. It can be placed directly over a gas flame or on an **electric hotplate**. Its main advantage is that it can be transferred to the table, where it will keep food hot during the meal. Substitute with an earthenware casserole pot or a Dutch oven.

hangiri

Omelet pan: The Japanese omelet pan is usually square-shaped, about 1 inch (3 cm) deep, traditionally used for making sushi omelets. It can be substituted by a conventional round skillet about 10 inches (25 cm) in diameter; trim the sides of the omelet once it has been cooked to make it square.

shamoji

Rice-cooling bowl (*hangiri*): This low, wide wooden bowl is used to cool cooked rice to give it the desired texture. The wider the bowl, the better to separate the rice grains.

Rice paddle (*shamoji*): The wooden rice scoop is used to spread cooked rice in the *hangiri* to cool. It traditionally represents domestic authority; whoever controls the *shamoji* in a Japanese household is in charge of the household affairs.

hone nuki

Basic Japanese Ingredients

Agar-agar (*kanten*) is a gelatin made from seaweed and can be purchased as strands, sticks, flakes or powder. It is commonly used to thicken ice cream, jelly and pudding. It is readily available in the dried foods section.

Bamboo shoots must first be peeled, sliced and simmered for 30 minutes till tender, before use. If using canned bamboo shoots, it is best to boil them in water for 5 minutes before preparing. Canned bamboo shoots are available at most grocery stores, however, Chinese grocery stores often carry the fresh shoots packed in plastic pouches.

Burdock root is a long, skinny root enjoyed more for its texture than its flavor. After scraping off the skin, it should be put into water immediately to prevent discoloring. Also available canned. If available fresh, it has a rough, dark grey exterior. Only the roots are used for food.

Chinese olive vegetable is available as a pickle, served as an accompaniment to sushi.

Crab sticks are long, narrow cylinders of compressed seafood that are intended as an inexpensive substitute to king crab legs. Sold in some supermarkets and Japanese fish stores.

Daikon is a large white radish often eaten raw—sliced or grated—with sashimi and tempura. It is also pickled and sold in jars. Daikon is readily available in most supermarkets.

Dashi **stock** is the basic Japanese fish broth made from water, *konbu* (dried kelp) and bonito flakes (page 16); it is also available in an instant version in packets. This is very useful when a small amount of stock is required for sauces and as a seasoning.

Dried bonito flakes (*katsuo bushi*) are sold in plastic packs in Asian food stores; larger flakes are used to make Basic Dashi Stock (page 16) whereas the finer ones are used as a garnish.

Fish sauce is a fermented fish product made by layering fish and salt in large jars and then siphoning off the liquid. It is sold bottled and is a common seasoning in Thai and Vietnamese food.

Furikake is a topping for rice dishes; it comprises toasted seaweed, sesame seeds, ground dried fish and salt.

Ginger is widely used in Japanese recipes. Fresh ginger is always used instead of ground ginger, which has a very different taste. Young ginger is preferred as it is more tender and juicy. Pickled Ginger (page 40) is a popular accompaniment to sushi and sashimi.

Glutinous rice is a variety of rice that becomes very sticky when cooked. Mainly used in snacks, sweets and desserts. This rice must be washed thoroughly and soaked overnight before steaming. Also available as finely milled glutinous rice flour.

Green tea powder (*matcha*) is readily available from Asian food stores. It is great for making Green Tea Ice Cream (page 126).

Japanese cucumbers are small and do not have the coarse seeds or high water content of Western cucumbers. Substitute baby cucumbers or pickling gherkins.

Jellyfish is generally sold as salted or dried strips; it is commonly used in vinegared salads. It is sold in plastic packages in the refrigerator section of supermarkets.

Kanpyo are long, thin, dried gourd strips used in sushi and slow-cooked dishes; also for tying food together.

Konbu is a dried kelp in the form of flat sheets with white powder on the surface, used to flavor Sushi Rice (pages 12-13) and Basic Dashi Stock (page 16). The kelp's flavor infuses quickly in water, so do not wash it before cooking—just wipe to remove any dust or powder. *Konbu* is often removed before a dish is served.

Lotus roots are the thick tubers of the aquatic lotus plant. It has a crunchy, powdery taste in its raw form. It is sold either covered in mud in the vegetable section, or cleaned and wrapped in plastic packets in the refrigerator section of the supermarket. A good substitute is jicama or cauliflower.

Mirin is a sweet cooking wine made by mixing steamed glutinous rice with distilled spirits and sugar. The resulting liquid contains 12% to 14% alcohol. Avoid products labeled "*aji-mirin*" as they are a MSG-flavored version.

Miso is an important seasoning in Japan—a fermented paste made from soybeans and rice, wheat or barley. It is available in various colors and flavors, but the most common are red and white misos, which are used in miso soups. Readily available in Asian food stores.

Nori refers to the dried leaves of a seaweed called laver, and is generally sold in 8 x 7-in (20 x 17 cm) sheets and used for wrapping sushi or cut into strips as a garnish. Nori is best toasted to make it crisp and fragrant (see instructions on page 64). Also sold pretoasted and packed flat in bags.

Palm sugar varies in color from gold to dark brown and is made from the sap of the coconut or *aren* palm. It has a rich flavor similar to dark brown sugar, molasses or maple syrup, all of which make good substitutes. Available in Asian food stores in plastic containers or packets.

Ponzu is a dressing made from citrus juice (lemon, lime or orange) mixed with soy, sugar and vinegar. Available bottled but you can also make your own fresh using the recipe on page 15.

Prepared Japanese mustard is similar to English mustard, but hotter —it is a blend of ground mustard seeds without flour. It can be purchased in powdered form in small cans or as a ready-to-use paste in tubes.

Red beans (*azuki*) are small, red and oval in shape with a light, nutty flavor and a fairly thin skin. They are used to make red rice for auspicious occasions, or boiled and sweetened to make a sweet bean paste, which is the base for many Japanese desserts. Sold dried or as a sweetened paste in cans.

Rice vinegar is a light, mildly tangy vinegar brewed from rice. Its color varies from almost white to pale gold.

Sake is a brewed Japanese rice wine. Chinese rice wine or dry sherry may be substituted.

Sansho **pepper** is made from the ground seeds of the Japanese prickly ash plant. Available in small glass bottles in Asian food stores, it gives a hot flavor to fatty foods such as eel. Substitute dried Sichuan pepper or ground red cayenne pepper.

Sesame oil should be used sparingly as a seasoning and not for frying. It has a rich nutty flavor and fragrance. Available in most grocery stores. Japanese sesame oil is milder than Chinese, so when using the latter, you may want to dilute it with a bit of vegetable oil.

Sesame paste is made from toasted sesame seeds that are ground up like peanut butter, but unsweetened. Commonly available in Asian food stores. Substitute *tahini* or make your own by pan-roasting and then grinding the seeds in a food processor.

Sesame salt (*goma shio*) is a mixture of toasted black sesame seeds (either whole or ground) and salt, and is a popular Japanese condiment.

Sesame seeds are available either white or black and are often pan-roasted (page 79) and sprinkled over cooked foods for added flavor.

Seven-spice chili mix is a potent blend of ground chili with other seasonings such as mustard, *sansho* pepper, black sesame and poppy seeds. It is often sprinkled on noodles, grilled items and one-pot dishes.

Shiitake mushrooms, also known as Chinese black mushrooms, are sold fresh or dried. They have a dark brown outer skin, a beige inner flesh, and a slightly woody flavor. Dried shiitakes can be substituted for fresh ones; soak for 10 to 15 minutes in hot water until tender, then drain. Discard the stems.

Shirataki **noodles** are thin strings of *konnyaku*, a glutinous paste obtained from the starchy elephant foot plant. They are eaten in *sukiyaki* and other hotpots. Substitute mung bean vermicelli (glass noodles).

Shiso **leaves** (also known as perilla leaves) have a fresh, slightly minty flavor. They are served with sashimi (and should be eaten with it), made into tempura and used in various ways to garnish sushi. Substitute mint leaves. The buds are made into a strong-flavored condiment, and the very young buds are made into tempura.

Short-grain Japanese rice is now grown in California and can be readily purchased everywhere. The most common variety is *uruchi mai* or non-glutinous rice (see pages 12–13 for recipe for cooking Japanese rice). The glutinous variety, *mochi gome*, absorbs more water than regular rice and is much stickier. Uncooked rice should be stored in an airtight container at room temperature.

Smoked conger eel (*anago*) is lightly boiled, grilled and basted before serving. Available in the refrigerator section of Asian supermarkets.

Soba **noodles** are thin, light brown noodles, sold fresh or in dried bundles. Follow the directions on the packet when boiling and rinse in cold water after cooking to remove the starch. Substitute buck wheat spaghetti.

in many Asian food stores. When cut in half, these slices serve as food pouches (pages 48, 51).

Somen noodles are very fine, flat wheat noodles normally sold in dried sticks. Boil until cooked but still firm, then rinse in cold water to remove the starch. Substitute ramen or angel hair pasta.

Soy sauce (*shoyu*) is fermented from soya beans and salt, and commonly used in marinades, sauces and dips. Substitute normal Chinese soy sauce.

Tezu vinegared water (page 12) is used for moistening the fingers when making sushi to prevent the rice from sticking to them.

Thai chili sauce is used mainly as a dipping sauce. Some sauces are sweeter than others and go particularly well with either chicken or seafood, and are so labeled. Available in bottles or jars.

Tofu (soybean curd) is available in various forms. **Firm tofu** has a slightly stronger and more sour flavor; **soft tofu** crumbles easily but has a more silky texture and refined flavor. **Tofu skin** is the thin layer of soy protein that forms on the surface of soybean milk when boiled to make tofu. The dried variety (**tofu sheet**) is produced when the film-like layer is skimmed and dried. **Deep-fried tofu slices** (*abura-age*) must be blanched before serving. Seasoned tofu slices are now available in cans or frozen packets

Udon noodles are thick, round, whitish-beige wheat noodles. Boil until cooked but still firm, then rinse to remove the starch; finally, reheat and serve *al dente*. Substitute Chinese wheat noodles or angel hair pasta.

Wakame is a type of seaweed available in dried strips. Soak in water for 5 to 10 minutes before using. Also sold seasoned and packed in plastic, in the refrigerator section of the supermarket.

Wasabi (Japanese horseradish) is unrelated to Western horseradish but produces a similarly sharp, biting effect on the tongue and in the nose. It is used to season sushi and is commonly available in a powdered form that can be reconstituted by mixing with warm water to form a thick paste. The mixture should be allowed to stand for about 10 minutes to let the flavors develop. If you can find it, freshly grated wasabi root has a much more intense flavor.

Buying Fish for Sashimi and Sushi

The most important consideration when selecting fish to use for sushi and sashimi is freshness. Quite simply, if the fish and seafood used are not extremely fresh, then the sushi and sashimi will not be good.

For shellfish—both hard and soft-shelled—extremely fresh usually means alive at the time of purchase and kept alive until required.

The types of fish and seafood most commonly used in Japan are mentioned here, but these should only act as a guide. Most fish can be eaten raw so we recommend that you use whatever available fresh fish is in season.

As a rule, frozen fish should be avoided when preparing dishes to be eaten raw. This is not only due to the health risk associated with fish that is less than fresh, but also because the flavor and texture are usually compromised. A generally accepted exception to this rule is tuna and squid which have been flash-frozen. If your fishmonger can guarantee that the fish has been treated in this manner, then you will probably find it to be a satisfactory substitute.

Some fish and seafood are precooked before being used in sushi and sashimi, such as shrimp, crab or lobster. Salmon is often smoked or salted; octopus and eel are often boiled or marinated. For sashimi, only the best parts or cuts are normally used. For example, the body of a squid (and not the tentacles) and only the prime fillets of a tuna are used.

Cutting Tips

Fish and seafood are usually cut into long, thin strips and pieces for sushi and sashimi. Use a long, thin, very sharp knife for cutting raw fish. Handle the fish as little as possible, by cutting each slice in a single motion, without sawing back and forth, as the friction will warm up the fish. Similarly, use the knife blade to lift or move slices on the cutting board or to place on the serving plate instead of your hands which will also warm up the fish.

Ideally, fish should be sliced as thinly as possible, and this is usually determined by the firmness of the fish. The firmer the fish, the thinner it can and should be sliced.

Ways of Cutting Fish

Paper-thin sashimi slices
Fish must be very fresh. Fillet can also be refrigerated for 10 minutes before slicing. Hold the fillet with one hand. Incline the knife at a 45° angle and slice very thinly, about $^1/_8$ in (3 mm), from the left to the right of the fish.

Thin sushi slices
Cut the fillet crosswise into $^1/_8$-in to $^1/_4$-in (3–6-mm) thick slices. Depending on the thickness of the fillet, these may be rectangular slices, bars or strips.

Cubes
Cut thick, soft-fleshed fish into $^3/_4$-in (2-cm) cubes by cutting fillet crosswise into $^3/_4$-in (2-cm) strips, and then cutting these strips into $^3/_4$-in (2-cm) pieces.

Strips
Cut very thin fillets diagonally or crosswise into strips $^3/_4$-in to 2-in (2-5 cm) wide and no longer than 2 in (5 cm) long. These strips (or threads) are then piled into a mound for serving.

How to Prepare Basic Sushi Rice

Short-grain Japanese rice is readily available in Asian markets, and usually includes the word "rose" in its name, e.g. "Japan Rose" or "California Rose"; it may also simply be labeled "Japanese Rice". Although often referred to as glutinous or sticky rice, the variety most commonly eaten by the Japanese—*uruchi mai*—is non-glutinous; the slight stickiness is due to the larger amount of water used during cooking.

1¹/₄ cups (250 g)
   uncooked short-grain
   Japanese rice
Cold water to wash rice
3-in (8-cm) square piece
   konbu (dried kelp)
1¹/₄ cups (300 ml) water
1 tablespoon sake
1 tablespoon rice vinegar
1 tablespoon sugar
1 teaspoon salt

Makes 2¹/₂ cups
Preparation time: **10 mins**
Cooking time: **15 mins**

Tezu (vinegared water)
When making sushi, *tezu* is used to moisten the fingers to prevent the rice from sticking to them.

¹/₂ cup (125 ml) water
1 tablespoon (15 ml) rice vinegar

Mix the two ingredients and use as required.

1 Place the rice in a large bowl or saucepan and add enough cold water to cover. Stir the rice with your fingers for 1 minute until the water becomes quite cloudy. Drain in a colander and repeat the process 3 or 4 times until the water is almost clear. Drain in a colander and set aside for at least 1 hour.

2 Wipe the *konbu* with a damp cloth to remove any grit, but do not try to wipe off the white powder. Using scissors, cut the *konbu* into 4 pieces.

3 Place the rice in a heavy-based saucepan. Add the water and sake, and place the *konbu* pieces on top. Cook over medium heat and remove the *konbu* just before it reaches boiling point (otherwise the rice becomes slimy). When the broth reaches a rolling boil, reduce heat to low, cover the saucepan, and simmer for about 15 minutes, or until all the liquid is absorbed. (Try not to lift the lid too many times to check this).

4 Remove from the heat; leave covered for 15 minutes. Using a wooden spoon or rice paddle, gently fold the rice to fluff it up. Place a kitchen towel over the saucepan and cover with the lid. Leave for 10 minutes to absorb excess moisture. Dissolve the sugar and salt with the vinegar in a small, non-metal bowl. Spread the rice out to dry in a large, non-metal shallow container, about 12 in (30 cm) across, and sprinkle on the vinegar mixture.

5 Fold the vinegared-rice gently with one hand while fanning the rice with the other. An electric fan can also be used. Continue fanning and folding the rice until it reaches room temperature, about 5 minutes. This quick cooling process is essential to achieve the desired texture, consistency and flavor of Sushi Rice.

6 Cover the container with a damp kitchen towel. The rice is now ready to be used and can be kept for up to 4 hours. Do not refrigerate the rice as this hardens and dries the grains.

Basic Japanese Dips and Sauces

Soy Dipping Sauce

Soy sauce
Dash of sesame paste (page 7) or wasabi (optional)

1 Japanese-style soy is the most basic of all dipping sauces. It may also be mixed with a little sesame paste or wasabi for added flavor.

Tempura Dipping Sauce

1 cup (250 ml) Basic Dashi Stock (page 16) or $^1/_2$ teaspoon
  instant *dashi* granules dissolved in 1 cup (250 ml) boiling water
4 tablespoons soy sauce
3 tablespoons *mirin*
3 teaspoons freshly grated daikon
3 teaspoons freshly grated ginger

1 Combine all ingredients in a bowl and stir well to mix.

Sesame Seed Sauce

$^3/_4$ cup (100 g) white sesame seeds, toasted
1 tablespoon miso
1 tablespoon sugar
2 tablespoons *mirin*
2 tablespoons rice vinegar
2 tablespoons sake
6 tablespoons soy sauce
1 teaspoon prepared Japanese mustard
3 tablespoons Basic Dashi Stock (page 16) or $^1/_4$ teaspoon instant
  dashi granules dissolved in 3 tablespoons boiling water

1 Combine all the ingredients in a bowl and blend until smooth.

Mustard Sauce

$^1/_4$ cup (60 ml) soy sauce
1 tablespoon sugar
1 teaspoon freshly grated ginger
2 teaspoons prepared Japanese mustard

1 Combine all the ingredients in a bowl and blend until smooth.

Ponzu Sauce

$^1/_4$ cup (60 ml) lemon juice
$^1/_4$ cup (60 ml) soy sauce
3 tablespoons Basic Dashi Stock (page 16) or $^1/_4$ teaspoon
   instant *dashi* granules dissolved in 3 tablespoons boiling water
1 tablespoon *mirin*

1 Combine all the ingredients in a bowl and stir well.

Homemade Japanese Mayonnaise

3 whole eggs
1 teaspoon prepared Japanese mustard
Salt and black pepper to taste
3 tablespoons lime juice
1 clove garlic, crushed
2 cups (500 ml) light vegetable oil, not canola

1 Combine the eggs, mustard, salt, pepper, lime juice, and
crushed garlic and process until light and frothy. Then
gradually add the oil while processing, until the mayonnaise is thick.
2 Transfer to a storage jar, refrigerate, and use as required.

Sesame Salt (Goma Shio)

1 tablespoon black sesame seeds
2 teaspoons salt

1 Dry-roast the sesame seeds in a skillet until they splatter. Transfer the toasted
seeds to a bowl and coat in the salt. Let cool and use as needed.

Coriander Pesto

2 cloves garlic, peeled
1 oz (30 g) macadamia nuts or pine nuts
Juice from $^1/_2$ lemon
1 cup (50 g) coriander leaves (cilantro) and stems
Salt and black pepper, to taste
$^1/_4$ cup (60 ml) oil

1 Combine the garlic, nuts, lemon juice, coriander leaves, salt and pepper, and
process. Drizzle the oil through the funnel to form a smooth, light paste. Do not
over process.
2 Pour into a clean airtight jar, smooth down the top, and cover surface with a thin
layer of oil. Seal and refrigerate until required.

Basic Dashi Stock (Bonito Flake Stock)

4-in (10-cm) square piece konbu (dried kelp), wiped clean
4 cups (1 liter) water
$^1/_4$ cup (60 ml) cold water
2 cups (20 g) bonito flakes

Yields 1 liter (4 cups)
Preparation time: 5 mins
Cooking time: 20 mins

1 Cut the *konbu* into 4 uniform strips. Place in a saucepan with the water and cook over medium heat. Just before it boils, remove from the heat and discard the *konbu*.

2 Add the cold water and bonito flakes. Bring to a boil, then remove from the heat and set aside to cool.

3 When the bonito flakes have sunk to the bottom, strain the liquid and discard the flakes. Store in a sealed jar in the fridge and use as needed.

Steamed Egg Custard (Chawan Mushi)

8 oz (250 g) chicken breast, cubed
1 tablespoon sake
1 teaspoon soy sauce
8 medium shrimp
4 large fresh shiitake mushrooms
1 small carrot, peeled and thinly sliced, each slice quartered
2 cups (125 g) spinach, rinsed
Zest of $^1/_4$ lemon, finely grated, to garnish

Dashi Custard
$2^1/_2$ cups (625 ml) Basic Dashi Stock (page 16) or $1^1/_4$ teaspoons instant *dashi* granules dissolved in $2^1/_2$ cups (625 ml) boiling water
1 tablespoon sake
1 teaspoon soy sauce
1 teaspoon salt
4 large eggs

1 Marinate the chicken in the sake and soy sauce for 10 minutes. Drain and set aside. Blanch and chop the spinach. Peel and devein the shrimp, leaving the tails intact. Discard the stems of the shiitake mushrooms and quarter the caps.

2 For the custard, heat the *dashi* stock with the sake, soy sauce and salt until the salt is dissolved. Remove from the heat. In a large bowl, combine the eggs without beating. Stir in the *dashi* mixture in a slow, steady stream and strain the egg mixture through a fine sieve.

3 Evenly distribute the chicken, shrimp and vegetables into 4 small heatproof bowls. Pour the custard over the contents, leaving a $^3/_4$-inch (2-cm) gap at the top of each bowl. Cover the bowl with a foil or lid.

4 Heat water in a large saucepan with a steamer rack and place the custard cups on the rack. Cover the steamer partially with a lid to allow the steam to escape. Steam over medium to high heat for 1 minute, then reduce heat to low and steam for another 15 minutes, until a knife comes out clean when inserted in the custard. Remove the custard cups from the steamer, garnish with the lemon zest, and serve immediately.

Serves 4
Preparation time: 15 mins
Cooking time: 15 mins

Healthy Miso Soup with Daikon

1 cup (125 g) daikon, peeled and sliced
4 cups (1 liter) Basic Dashi Stock (page 16) or 2 teaspoons instant *dashi* granules dissolved in 4 cups (1 liter) boiling water
3 tablespoons miso
8 green beans, cut into lengths
1 teaspoon soy sauce (optional)

1 Slice the daikon lengthwise into quarters, then into $1/8$-in (3-mm) slices as shown below.
2 Place the daikon and *dashi* stock in a saucepan over medium heat and cook until the daikon softens, about 2 minutes.
3 Place the miso in a small bowl and ladle some of the hot *dashi* stock over it. Stir with a wooden spoon until the miso is dissolved, and pour the dissolved miso into the soup.
4 Stir in the beans and soy sauce, then bring the soup to a boil and immediately remove from the heat. Ladle the soup into 4 bowls and serve.

Serves 4
Preparation time: **5 mins**
Cooking time: **5 mins**

Cut the daikon in quarters, lengthwise, then slice into $1/8$-in (3-mm) thickness.

Cut the green beans into lengths.

Stir miso and dashi stock with a wooden spoon until miso is well dissolved.

Stir in beans and soy sauce, then bring to a boil and remove from heat.

Flavorful Clear Soup with Shrimp

8 medium shrimp, peeled and deveined, tails intact
4 cups (1 liter) Basic Dashi Stock (page 16) or 2 teaspoons instant *dashi* granules dissolved in 4 cups (1 liter) boiling water
2 okra, cut in $^1/_4$-in ($^1/_2$-cm) slices
1 teaspoon soy sauce
Zest of $^1/_4$ lemon, finely grated, to garnish

1 Warm the *dashi* stock in a saucepan and adjust seasoning with salt, if required. Bring to a boil over medium heat and add the shrimp. Reduce heat and simmer for 1 to 2 minutes, until the shrimp turns pink. Add the okra and soy sauce and remove from the heat.

2 Place 2 shrimp in each serving bowl and ladle the soup over them. Garnish with the lemon zest and serve.

Serves 4
Preparation time: **15 mins**
Cooking time: **5 mins**

Clear Soup with Scallops and Asparagus

4 cups (1 liter) Basic Dashi Stock (page 16) or 2 teaspoons instant *dashi* granules dissolved in 4 cups (1 liter) boiling water
Zest of 1/4 lemon, finely grated
1 teaspoon salt
4 asparagus spears, tough ends discarded
8 fresh scallops, cleaned with muscle removed
1 teaspoon soy sauce

1 Place the *dashi* stock, half of the lemon zest and salt in a saucepan and bring almost to a boil, then reduce heat immediately. Remove the zest with a sieve and discard.

2 Cut the asparagus spears in half and add to the saucepan. Bring to a boil and reduce heat.

3 Add the scallops and soy sauce, stir, and simmer over low heat for another minute until the asparagus and scallops are done. Remove from the heat.

4 Serve in 4 individual serving bowls and garnish with the remaining lemon zest.

Serves 4
Preparation time: **10 mins**
Cooking time: **4 mins**

Miso Soup with Tofu and Bamboo Shoots

4 cups (1 liter) Basic
Dashi Stock (page 16)
or 2 teaspoons instant
dashi granules
dissolved in 4 cups
(1 liter) boiling water
1 cup (100 g) fresh or
canned bamboo shoots,
cut into matchsticks
6 oz (175 g) soft tofu,
cubed
3 tablespoons miso

Serves 4
Preparation time: **5 mins**
Cooking time: **5 mins**

1 Place the *dashi* stock and bamboo shoots in a saucepan and bring to a boil over medium heat. Reduce heat to low and simmer for 1 minute, then add the tofu.

2 Place the miso in a bowl or large ladle and dissolve it with some of the hot soup, stirring with a wooden spoon. Pour the dissolved miso into the saucepan.

3 Increase the heat and bring the soup to almost a boil, then remove from the heat. Ladle the soup into 4 bowls and serve immediately.

Miso Soup with Tofu and Mushrooms

4 cups (1 liter) Basic Dashi Stock (page 16) or 2 teaspoons instant *dashi* granules dissolved in 4 cups (1 liter) boiling water

4 fresh shiitake mushrooms, stems discarded, caps cut into ½-in (1-cm) sections,

6 oz (175 g) soft tofu, cubed

4 tablespoons miso

Soy sauce to taste

1 Bring the *dashi* stock almost to a boil in a saucepan and add the sliced mushrooms. Reduce heat and simmer the mushrooms for 1 minute, then add the tofu. Reduce heat to very low.

2 Place the miso in a small bowl and ladle some of the hot *dashi* stock over it. Stir with a wooden spoon until the miso is well dissolved. Pour the dissolved miso into the saucepan.

3 Stir in the soy sauce and return the soup to almost a boil. Remove from the heat immediately, ladle the soup into 4 soup bowls, and serve.

Serves 4
Preparation time: **20 mins**
Cooking time: **10 mins**

Tofu and Vegetable Soup

1 cup (250 ml) water
1 teaspoon vinegar
4 oz (125 g) burdock root, peeled (optional)
8 oz (250 g) firm tofu
1 teaspoon oil
1 teaspoon sesame oil
4 oz (125 g) ground chicken
1 potato, peeled, quartered and thinly sliced
1 cup (125 g) daikon, peeled, quartered and thinly sliced
1 carrot, peeled, quartered and thinly sliced
5 cups (1$^1/_4$ liters) Basic Dashi Stock (page 16) or 2$^1/_2$ teaspoons instant *dashi* granules dissolved in 5 cups (1$^1/_4$ liters) boiling water
1 tablespoon soy sauce
1 teaspoon salt
4 fresh shiitake mushrooms, quartered
2 spring onions, cut into sections
Seven-spice chili mix or *sansho* pepper

1 Combine the water and vinegar in a mixing bowl. Shave the burdock root into thin, long strips and soak in the vinegar-water mixture for 5 to 10 minutes. Rinse and drain.
2 Using a fork, break the tofu roughly into chunks.
3 Heat both the oils in a saucepan over medium heat, and when hot, add the chicken. Stir-fry the chicken, until just cooked, about 1 minute.
4 Add the burdock root, potato, daikon and carrot, and stir-fry for another 2 minutes.
5 Add the *dashi* stock, soy sauce and salt, and bring to a boil. Reduce heat to low and simmer until the vegetables are tender, about 4 minutes. Stir the mushrooms and tofu into the soup, and simmer for another 2 minutes. Add the spring onions and remove from the heat. Serve immediately with the seven-spice chili mix or *sansho* pepper.

Serves 4
Preparation time: **20 mins**
Cooking time: **12 mins**

Chicken Meatballs in Clear Soup

1 lb (450 g) ground chicken
2 spring onions, thinly sliced
1 tablespoon freshly grated ginger
$^1/_4$ cup (60 ml) soy sauce
1 medium egg
2 tablespoons cornstarch
3 cups (750 ml) Basic Dashi Stock (page 16) or 1$^1/_2$
    teaspoons instant *dashi* granules dissolved in 3 cups
    (750 ml) boiling water
2 tablespoons sake
2 tablespoons *mirin*
1 spring onion, thinly sliced, to garnish
Fresh coriander leaves (cilantro), to garnish

1 Combine the ground chicken, spring onions, ginger,
1 tablespoon of the soy sauce, and egg in a mixing
bowl. Sprinkle in the cornstarch and mix well.
2 Shape the chicken mixture into meatballs about 2 in
(5 cm) in diameter. You may need to moisten your
hands with water to prevent the mixture from sticking.
3 Combine the *dashi* stock, sake, *mirin* and the
remaining soy sauce in a saucepan and bring to a boil
over medium heat. Reduce heat immediately.
4 Add the chicken balls, one at a time, to the simmering broth, and cook for about 5 minutes. Remove the
meatballs from the broth with a slotted spoon and
serve in 4 individual serving bowls. Pour the broth
over them and garnish with the spring onion and
coriander leaves.

Serves 4
Preparation time: **5 mins**
Cooking time: **15 mins**

Chicken and Egg Drop Soup

4 oz (125 g) chicken breast, cut into thin strips
1 tablespoon sake
$1/2$ teaspoon salt
4 cups (1 liter) Basic Dashi Stock (page 16) or 2 teaspoons instant *dashi* granules dissolved in 4 cups (1 liter) boiling water
1 teaspoon soy sauce
2 eggs, beaten
8 thin slices carrot, blanched, to garnish

1 Place the chicken strips in a small bowl and marinate in the sake and $1/4$ teaspoon of the salt for 5 to 10 minutes.
2 Bring the *dashi* stock to a boil in a saucepan. Reduce heat and add $1/4$ teaspoon salt, soy sauce and the chicken, and simmer for 1 minute.
3 Slowly pour one-third of the beaten egg into the soup, stirring constantly; the egg will form "threads" as it enters the broth. When the soup boils again, add another one-third of the egg, stirring constantly. Bring the soup back to a boil, add the rest of the egg and when all the egg is cooked, remove from the heat.
4 Ladle the soup into 4 serving bowls and garnish with the carrot. Serve immediately.

Serves 4
Preparation time: **20 mins**
Cooking time: **15 mins**

Fresh Cold Tofu Appetizer

4 *shiso* leaves, stems discarded
1 lb (450 g) soft tofu, drained on a rack for 30 minutes or patted dry with paper toweling to remove moisture
2 tablespoons soy sauce
2 spring onions, thinly sliced
1/4 cup bonito flakes
2 tablespoons freshly grated ginger

1 Stack the *shiso* leaves and cut them into thin, long strips lengthwise, about 1/8-in (3-mm) wide.
2 Cut the tofu into 4 equal pieces and place them in a serving bowl.
3 Serve the soy sauce in 4 small individual dipping bowls.
4 Sprinkle the sliced *shiso* leaves, spring onions and bonito flakes over the tofu. Place a small mound of the ginger on the side, and serve immediately with the soy sauce.

Serves 4
Preparation time: **5 mins**
Assembling time: **3 mins**

Sesame Omelet

2 large eggs
$1/_4$ teaspoon salt
$1/_4$ teaspoon freshly
  ground black pepper
1 tablespoon oil
2 tablespoons white or
  black sesame seeds

Makes 1 large omelet
Preparation time: **5 mins**
Cooking time: **5 mins**

1 Gently combine the eggs in a bowl with the salt and pepper . Do not overmix as this will make the omelet tough.
2 Using a pastry brush, lightly brush the inside of a large omelet pan with the oil. Heat the omelet pan over medium heat and pour in the egg mixture.
3 Tilt the pan to cover the bottom with the egg, and using a spatula, swirl the egg around to allow it to cook.
4 When the omelet is almost set, sprinkle with the sesame seeds. Flip the omelet over and allow the seeds to toast for 1 minute.
5 Slide the omelet from the pan onto a plate or cutting board.

Sesame Omelet with Shrimp

10 medium shrimp,
  peeled and deveined
1 cup (250 ml) water
3 tablespoons Home-
  made Japanese
  Mayonnaise (page 15)
$1/_2$ teaspoon freshly
  ground black pepper
1 Sesame Omelet
  (see above)
$1/_2$ teaspoon fish sauce
4 sprigs watercress

Makes 10–12 slices
Preparation time: **5 mins**
Cooking time: **10 mins**
Assembling time: **10 mins**

1 Boil the shrimp in the water for 3 to 4 minutes, until they turn pink. Remove and let cool. Slice the shrimp into small chunks and mix with the mayonnaise and black pepper.
2 Lay the Sesame Omelet on a flat work surface and spread the shrimp mixture across the center of the omelet. Sprinkle the fish sauce over the shrimp mixture, and place the watercress sprigs in a line across the middle.
3 Carefully roll up the omelet. Wrap it in plastic wrap and refrigerate for about 10 minutes to help it retain its shape before slicing into 10 or 12 pieces.

Rice and Mushroom Egg Parcels

4 shiitake mushrooms
2 batches Sesame Omelet
(page 30), omitting
sesame seeds
1 clove garlic, crushed
2 tablespoons soy sauce
1 cup (150 g) cooked Sushi
Rice (pages 12–13)
1 spring onion, sliced
$1/4$ teaspoon salt
$1/4$ teaspoon freshly
ground black pepper

Makes 6 parcels
Preparation time: **20 mins**
Cooking time: **20 mins**
Assembling time: **15 mins**

1 If using dried mushrooms, soak them in hot water to soften, about 20 minutes. Drain the mushrooms and squeeze out any excess moisture.

2 Make 6 small omelets in a small skillet. Stack the omelets on top of each other and cover with a cloth to prevent them from drying out.

3 Discard the mushroom stems and dice the caps. Combine the garlic and soy sauce in a bowl and marinate the mushrooms for at least 15 minutes.

4 Drain the mushrooms and combine with the Sushi Rice and spring onion in a mixing bowl. Season with the salt and black pepper.

5 Place the omelets on a flat work surface and spoon 2 tablespoons of the mushroom-rice mixture onto each one. Fold in the sides to form a flat, square parcel and place seam side down on a serving platter.

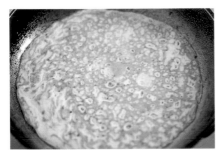
Make the omelets in a small skillet.

Discard the stems and dice the mushroom caps.

Combine the rice, diced mushrooms, salt and black pepper in a small bowl.

Fold in the sides of the omelet to form a flat, square parcel; place it seam side down.

Sesame Omelet with Shiitake Mushrooms

6 fresh shiitake mushrooms, stems discarded
1 teaspoon soy sauce
1 teaspoon sesame oil
1 teaspoon lemon juice
1 teaspoon *mirin*
1 tablespoon olive oil
1 Sesame Omelet (page 30)
1 spring onion, thinly sliced
$^1/_2$ green bell pepper, very thinly sliced

1 Slice the mushrooms across, very finely.
2 Combine the soy sauce, sesame oil, lemon juice and *mirin,* and set aside.
3 Heat the olive oil in a small skillet and sauté the mushrooms until soft, about 2 minutes. Remove from the heat and pour the soy mixture over the mushrooms. Stir well and allow to cool completely.
4 Place the Sesame Omelet on a flat work surface, with the seeds facing down. Place the cooled mushroom mixture across the center of the omelet. Sprinkle with the spring onion and bell pepper.
5 Roll the omelet over the filling, to form a cylinder with the filling in the middle.
6 Slice the omelet into quarters at an angle to serve as appetizers, or slice into 10 to 12 smaller rounds for hors d'oeuvres as shown.

Makes 4 large or 10–12 small rolls
Preparation time: **5 mins**
Cooking time: **10 mins**
Assembling time: **10 mins**

Sesame Spinach Sushi

4 large eggs
$^1/_2$ teaspoon salt
$^1/_2$ teaspoon freshly
  ground black pepper
2 tablespoons oil
2 hard-boiled eggs,
  shelled and diced
1 cup (150 g) cooked
  Sushi Rice (pages 12–13)
$^1/_4$ teaspoon salt
$^1/_4$ teaspoon freshly
  ground black pepper
$^1/_2$ sheet *nori*, toasted
  (see page 64), cut into
  6 strips

Sesame Spinach
2 tablespoons white
  sesame seeds, toasted
4 cups (10 oz/300 g)
  fresh spinach leaves
$^1/_2$ teaspoon sugar
Large pinch of salt
2 tablespoons *Dashi*
  Stock (page 16) or $^1/_4$
  teaspoon instant *dashi*
  granules dissolved in 2
  tablespoons boiling
  water
1 tablespoon soy sauce

1 Wash the spinach leaves and set aside to drain.
2 To prepare the Sesame Spinach, grind the sesame seeds until smooth with a mortar and pestle. Heat the sugar, salt, *dashi* stock, soy sauce and the ground seeds in a large saucepan over high heat. Toss in the spinach, one handful at a time until all the spinach is just cooked. Remove from the heat and drain. Set aside to use as a filling for the sushi, or serve immediately as a side dish garnished with toasted sesame seeds.
3 To make the egg wrappers for the sushi, mix the eggs, salt and pepper together in a bowl. Cook one-sixth of the egg mixture in an omelet pan using 1 teaspoon of oil. Do the same with the rest of the egg mixture to make 6 small omelets. Stack the omelets on top of each other and cover with a cloth to prevent them from drying out.
4 Combine the diced hard-boiled eggs and spinach with the Sushi Rice. Season with salt and black pepper.
5 Place the omelets flat on a work surface and spoon 2 tablespoons of the egg and spinach mixture onto each. Gather up the edges of the omelet and tie with a thin strip of *nori* to form a parcel. Repeat to form 6 parcels.

Makes 6 parcels
Preparation time: **20 mins**
Cooking time: **20 mins**

Grind sesame seeds in a mortar and pestle until smooth.

Add the spinach to the saucepan a handful at a time, stirring constantly.

Chicken Rolls with Spring Onions

4 chicken thighs
(about 1 lb or 450 g)
1 teaspoon freshly grated
ginger
$^3/_4$ cup (175 ml) sake
2 tablespoons soy sauce
4 spring onions
2 teaspoons cornstarch
1 tablespoon oil
Kitchen string

Serves 4
Preparation time: 30 mins
Cooking time: 20 mins

1 Debone the chicken thighs and place them on a work surface with the skin side down. Score the flesh with a sharp knife. Press on the meat to spread it out, creating an even thickness.

2 Combine the ginger, 2 tablespoons of the sake, and the soy sauce in a bowl. Coat the chicken and set aside to marinate for 20 minutes, turning occasionally.

3 Drain the chicken and place it skin side down on a working surface, reserving the marinade. Cut the spring onions to the same length as the chicken and place 3 or 4 pieces across each piece of chicken. Sprinkle with an even coating of cornstarch.

4 Roll each piece of chicken up and fasten with the kitchen string, securing at both ends.

5 Heat the oil in a large skillet over medium to high heat. Place the chicken rolls seam side down and cook, turning frequently with tongs, until they are evenly browned.

6 Drain excess fat from the skillet, leaving the chicken in, and add the remaining sake. Reduce heat to medium -low, cover and simmer for 7 minutes.

7 Add the reserved marinade and cook the chicken roll for another 10 to 12 minutes, or until tender.

8 To serve, remove the string and slice the chicken crossways into $^3/_4$-in (2-cm)-thick slices and spoon the pan juices over the slices.

Place 3 or 4 spring onion sticks across each piece of chicken.

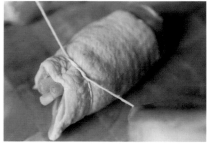

Roll up the chicken and fasten with string on both ends.

Pickled Ginger

$1/_2$ cup (125 g) fresh young ginger, peeled
   and thinly sliced diagonally
1 cup (250 ml) boiling water
$1/_2$ cup (125 ml) rice vinegar
2 tablespoons sugar
$1/_2$ teaspoon salt

1 Place the ginger slices in a small bowl and cover
with the boiling water. Leave to stand for 30 seconds
and drain well.
2 Combine the vinegar, sugar and salt in a small non-
metallic bowl and stir until the sugar completely dis-
solves. Add the drained ginger and coat well with the
mixture.
3 Cover the bowl with a plastic sheet and leave it to
stand for at least 1 hour, then refrigerate until well-
chilled and the ginger slices turn pink. To serve,
remove the ginger from the pickling liquid.

Simple Tuna Sashimi

1 teaspoon wasabi paste
Juice from 2 large limes
1 lb (450 g) fresh tuna fillet, thinly sliced
$1/_2$ cup (75 g) red radish, thinly sliced
4 tablespoons Pickled Ginger (see above)
4 sprigs fresh coriander leaves (cilantro)

1 To prepare the dressing, mix the wasabi paste with
the lime juice and set aside.
2 To arrange the sashimi, distribute the slices of tuna
onto 4 individual serving plates. Garnish with a small
mound of the radish, topped with the Pickled Ginger.
Sprinkle the tuna with the fresh coriander leaves and
drizzle with the prepared dressing. Serve immediately.

Serves 4
Preparation time: **1 hour**
Assembling time: **5 mins**

Traditional Seafood Sashimi Platter

$^1/_2$ cup (125 g) daikon, peeled and sliced into thin threads

Ice water

4 *shiso* leaves or other leafy greens

2 oz (60 g) green seaweed or salted greens, to garnish (optional)

5 oz (150 g) fresh tuna fillet, skinned

5 oz (150 g) fresh sea bream fillet or mackerel, skinned

1 fresh abalone or giant clam, shucked and cleaned

5 oz (150 g) fresh squid, skinned and cleaned

4 fresh scallops, about 3 oz (85 g)

5 oz (150 g) boiled octopus

1 tablespoon wasabi paste

4 tablespoons soy sauce or Ponzu Sauce (page 15)

1 Peel the daikon and leave it in the ice water until needed. Drain well before serving. Rinse the *shiso* leaves and seaweed in cold water. Pat dry with paper toweling.

2 To prepare the fish, trim the thin sides of the tuna and sea bream fillet to make a more rectangular shape if necessary. Cut into thin slices. Cut the abalone crosswise into $^1/_4$-in (6-mm) slices. Open the squid flat. Make cuts along the body about $2^1/_2$ in (6 cm) apart to make rectangles. Cut these rectangles across to make thin strips.

3 Slice the scallops to make 5 thin discs. Slice the boiled octopus into $^1/_4$-in (6-mm) slices.

4 Arrange all the seafood, garnish and wasabi paste on a serving platter. Pour the dipping sauce into small individual dipping bowls and serve immediately.

Serves 4
Preparation time: **30 mins**
Assembling time: **5 mins**

Nigiri Sushi with Shrimp, Tuna and Eel

6 medium shrimp, peeled and deveined, tails intact
Small bowl of ice water
1/4 cup (60 ml) rice vinegar
2 teaspoons sugar
8 oz (225 g) fresh tuna fillet, skinned
8 oz (225 g) smoked conger eel (*anago*, page 8)
Small bowl of *tezu* (page 12)
2 cups (300 g) cooked Sushi Rice (pages 12–13)
2 tablespoons wasabi paste
Pickled Ginger (page 40)
Soy Dipping Sauce (page 14)

Serves 4
Preparation time: **30 mins**
Assembling time: **40 mins**

1 Bring a saucepan of salted water to a boil. Insert a wooden skewer lengthwise into each shrimp from end to end to prevent the shrimp from curling during blanching. Blanch the shrimp for 30 seconds. Remove immediately and refresh in ice water.

2 Combine the vinegar and sugar in a small bowl. Add the shrimp and let it stand for 5 minutes, then drain.

3 Slide a knife lengthwise along the underside of the shrimp without cutting through. Open the shrimp flat, top side up; repeat with the remaining shrimp. Pat dry with paper toweling.

4 Cut the tuna fillet crosswise into 1 x 2-in (2 x 5-cm) pieces. Cut the eel into thin slices.

5 To shape the rice, first moisten hands with the *tezu* to avoid sticking, then take 1 tablespoon of the Sushi Rice in your right hand and shape to form an oval "finger". Pick up the tuna with your left hand and use your right index finger to dab a little wasabi on it. Place the rice "finger" on top of the tuna. Using your index finger, press the rice onto the tuna. Turn the rice and tuna over so that the tuna is on top. Using your index finger and middle finger, mold the tuna around the rice so that the rice does not show around the edges of the tuna. Repeat with the remaining tuna, shrimp and eel.

6 Arrange the Nigiri Sushi on a serving platter. Serve with Pickled Ginger and Soy Dipping Sauce.

Nigiri Sushi with Egg

Rolled Omelet

4 large eggs
5 tablespoons Basic
 Dashi Stock (page 16)
 or $1/4$ teaspoon instant
 dashi granules dis-
 solved in 5 table-
 spoons boiling water
2 tablespoons *mirin*
1 teaspoon sugar
Scant 1 teaspoon soy
 sauce
$1/4$ teaspoon salt
Oil for frying

Sushi

2 cups (300 g) cooked
 Sushi Rice (pages 12–13)
1 sheet *nori,* toasted
 (page 64) and cut into
 $1/2$-in (1-cm) wide
 strips
Small bowl of *tezu*
 (page 12)

Serves 4
Preparation time: **20 mins**
Cooking time: **15 mins**

1 To make the omelet, gently combine the eggs in a bowl with the *dashi* stock, *mirin*, sugar, soy sauce and salt. Stir until the sugar is dissolved.

2 Heat a regular skillet or omelet pan over medium heat and brush it lightly with the oil. Pour about one-third of the egg mixture into the skillet, tilting the skillet to cover the base. When the egg is set on the bottom but still moist on top, about 30 seconds, use a spatula or chopsticks to roll the egg up quickly but carefully. Leave the rolled omelet on one side of the skillet.

3 Brush the skillet with more of the oil and pour half of the remaining egg mixture into the skillet, again tilting the pan to cover the base. After 30 seconds, roll out the first omelet over the new one. Repeat with the remaining egg mixture.

4 Lift the final omelet onto a bamboo mat or kitchen towel and roll it up, gently squeezing out any excess moisture. Let it stand for 1 to 2 minutes. Serve immediately, garnished with sliced daikon mixed with a little soy, or use as a topping for sushi.

5 To use as a sushi topping, place the prepared rolled omelet on a board and flatten it slightly to make it more rectangular. Cut it crosswise into $1/2$-in (1-cm) slices.

6 Moisten hands with the *tezu.* Form rice "fingers" as in page 44. Repeat method of making sushi, using the omelet as the topping until all the Sushi Rice is used up.

7 Dampen 1 end of a *nori* strip and wrap it around the sushi like a belt. Repeat with the remaining ingredients.

Using a spatula or chopsticks, roll up the omelet to one side of the pan.

Pour new egg mixture into the pan then roll back the omelet in this new egg mixture.

Stuffed Tofu Pouches (Inari Sushi)

6 deep-fried tofu slices
  (*abura-age*, page 9)
1 cup (250 ml) Basic
  Dashi Stock (page 16)
  or ¹/₂ teaspoon instant
  dashi granules
  dissolved in 1 cup
  (250 ml) boiling water
2 tablespoons sake
2 tablespoons soy sauce
1¹/₂ tablespoons sugar
1 tablespoon *mirin*
Small bowl of *tezu*
  (page 12)
2 cups (300 g) cooked
  Sushi Rice (pages 12–13)
Black or white sesame
  seeds, toasted
4 tablespoons Pickled
  Ginger (page 40)
Soy Dipping Sauce
  (page 14)

1 Rinse the deep-fried tofu slices under boiling water for a few seconds to remove excess oil. Drain and pat dry with paper toweling.

2 Heat the *dashi* stock, sake, soy sauce, sugar and *mirin* in a saucepan and bring to a boil. Reduce heat, add the tofu slices and simmer for 10 minutes. Remove from the heat and drain.

3 Cut the tofu slices in half, either diagonally or crosswise, depending on the desired shape.

4 Moisten hands with the *tezu* to prevent rice from sticking. Open the tofu pouch and carefully insert 2 tablespoons of the Sushi Rice. Fold the edges of the pouch over the rice to seal it and place it seam side down on a serving plate.

5 Sprinkle with the sesame seeds and serve with the Pickled Ginger and Soy Dipping Sauce.

Makes 12 pouches
Preparation time: **10 mins**
Cooking time: **5 mins**
Assembling time: **10 mins**

Remove the tofu slices from the simmering liquid with a slotted spoon.

Slice the simmered tofu crosswise or diagonally.

Open the tofu pouch carefully and fill it with a little Sushi Rice.

Fold the edges of the pouch to seal it, then place it seam side down on a plate.

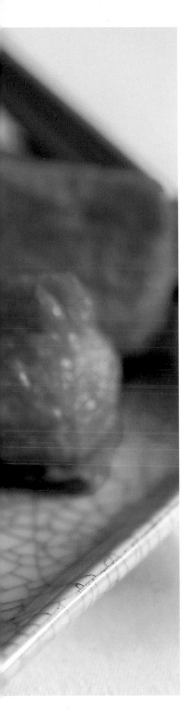

Crab Salad Tofu Pouches

6 deep-fried tofu slices (*abura-age*, page 9)
1 cup (250 ml) Basic Dashi Stock (page 16) or $^1/_2$ teaspoon instant *dashi* granules dissolved in 1 cup
(250 ml) boiling water
2 tablespoons sake
2 tablespoons soy sauce
1$^1/_2$ tablespoons sugar
1 tablespoon *mirin*
8 oz (225 g) cooked crab meat, picked clean
$^1/_2$ cup (125 ml) Homemade Japanese Mayonnaise
(page 15)
$^1/_2$ avocado, diced and sprinkled with lemon juice
2 to 3 water chestnuts, diced
2 tablespoons salmon roe or flying fish roe
Soy Dipping Sauce (page 14)

1 Rinse the tofu slices in boiling water for a few seconds to remove excess oil. Drain and pat dry with
paper toweling.
2 Heat the *dashi* stock, sake, soy sauce, sugar and *mirin*
in a saucepan and bring to a boil. Reduce heat, add the
tofu and simmer for 10 minutes. Remove from the
heat, drain and allow the tofu to cool completely.
3 Cut the tofu slices in half, either diagonally or
crosswise, depending on the desired shape.
4 Squeeze out any excess liquid from the crab meat
and combine with the mayonnaise. Pat dry the avocado
and water chestnuts before combining with the crab
mixture and the salmon roe. Gently fold the salad,
taking care not to break up the delicate ingredients.
5 Insert 2 teaspoons of the crab salad into the tofu
pouch. Flatten the base of the pouches and sit them
upright on a serving platter.

Makes 12 pouches
Preparation time: **10 mins**
Cooking time: **5 mins**
Assembling time: **10 mins**

Cucumber, Crab and Salmon Rolls
(Maki Sushi)

1 small cucumber, peeled
3 sheets *nori*, toasted (page 64) and halved
Small bowl of *tezu* (page 12)
3 cups (450 g) cooked Sushi Rice (pages 12–13)
2 tablespoons wasabi paste
2 tablespoons white sesame seeds, toasted
8 oz (225 g) salmon fillet, skinned and cut into thin strips
8 oz (225 g) cooked crab meat or crab sticks
$^1/_3$ cup (90 ml) soy sauce
$^3/_4$ cup Pickled Ginger (page 40)

Serves 4
Preparation time: **20 mins**
Assembling time: **30 mins**

1 To make the cucumber rolls, halve, then quarter the cucumber lengthwise into thin, long strips.

2 Place the bamboo mat on a work surface, facing you with the strips horizontal. Place a half sheet of the *nori* on the mat, shiny side down, with the edge of the *nori* $^3/_4$ in (2 cm) away from the edge of the mat closer to you.

3 To make the rolls, moisten your hands with the *tezu* to prevent the rice from sticking. Spread about $^1/_2$ cup (75 g) of the Sushi Rice onto the *nori* with your fingers, leaving a $^3/_4$-in (2-cm) space at the top of the *nori* sheet.

4 Dab some of the wasabi paste down the middle of the rice and place 2 to 3 pieces of the cucumber on the wasabi. Sprinkle 1 teaspoon of the sesame seeds on the rice.

5 To roll, hold the edge of the mat nearest to you with one hand, press fingers of the other hand over the cucumber to hold it in place and roll the mat over the rice, away from you. Lift up the top of the mat and turn the roll over a little so that the empty *nori* strip seals the sushi roll.

6 Unroll the bamboo mat and remove the sushi roll. Using a moist, very sharp knife, cut the roll into 6 to 8 uniform pieces. Repeat using the salmon and crab meat. Serve with the soy sauce and Pickled Ginger.

Place the nori on the bamboo mat $^3/_4$ in (2 cm) away from the edge closer to you.

Spread the rice evenly over the nori, leaving a $^3/_4$-in (2-cm) gap at the top.

Roll the bamboo mat over the rice, away from you.

Using a moist, very sharp knife, cut the roll into 6 to 8 pieces.

California Rolls

12 medium shrimp, peeled and deveined or 1 cup
 cooked crab meat
1 large avocado
Juice from half a lemon
4 sheets *nori*, toasted (page 64)
4 cups (600 g) cooked Sushi Rice (pages 12–13)
8 lettuce leaves, coarsely cut
3 tablespoons Homemade Japanese Mayonnaise
 (page 15) mixed with 1 teaspoon wasabi paste
3 tablespoons Pickled Ginger (page 40)
3 tablespoons salmon roe
1 tablespoon toasted sesame seeds

1 Poach the shrimp and set aside to cool.
2 Cut the avocado in half lengthwise. Remove the
flesh and cut into strips about $1/2$ in (1 cm), keeping
the pieces as long as possible. Drizzle with the lemon
juice to prevent discoloration.
3 To make the rolls, follow the directions for Maki
Sushi on page 52. Place 2 lettuce leaves down the
middle of the rice on each roll. Top with 3 shrimp,
placing them end to end along the center of the lettuce. Place the avocado strips end to end to form a
line next to the shrimp.
4 Spoon $1/4$ of the mayonnaise on the shrimp and add
some of the Pickled Ginger, salmon roe and sesame
seeds to the roll. Roll up like the Maki Sushi and cut
each roll into 8 slices.

Makes 32 slices
Preparation time: **15 mins**
Assembling time: **30 mins**

Ocean Trout California Rolls

8 oz (200 g) ocean trout fillets
$^1/_2$ cup pickled Chinese olive vegetable (page 5)
4 cups (600 g) cooked Sushi Rice (pages 12–13)
4 sheets *nori*, toasted (page 64)
2 tablespoons sliced capers
Dill cucumbers, peeled and cut into thin strips
3 tablespoons Homemade Japanese Mayonnaise (page 15)
1 tablespoon Dijon mustard

1 Cut the ocean trout fillet into strips about $^3/_4$-in (2-cm) thick.
2 Mix the olive vegetable into the Sushi Rice.
3 Follow the directions for making California Rolls (page 55), using the dill cucumbers, mayonnaise and Dijon mustard as a filling.

Makes 32 slices
Preparation time: **20 mins**
Assembling time: **30 mins**

Thai Shrimp California Rolls

12 medium shrimp, peeled and deveined
2 tablespoons lemon juice
2 tablespoons fish sauce
1 tablespoon palm sugar (page 7)
1 spring onion, thinly sliced
1 small chili, thinly sliced
4 cups (600 g) cooked Sushi Rice (pages 12–13)
4 sheets *nori*, toasted (page 64)
8 lettuce leaves, roughly sliced
Japanese cucumber, unpeeled and cut into strips
$^1/_2$ cup fresh coriander leaves (cilantro)

1 Marinate the shrimp in the lemon juice, fish sauce, palm sugar, spring onion and chili for 15 minutes.
2 Follow the directions for making California Rolls (page 55). Drain off excess liquid from the lettuce and place it over the middle of the prepared rice.
3 Place 3 shrimp end to end along the center of the rice, then add a strip of the Japanese cucumber and sprinkle with the fresh coriander leaves. Repeat until all the ingredients are used up.

Makes 32 slices
Preparation time: **20 mins**
Assembling time: **30 mins**

Lobster and Mango California Rolls

4 sheets *nori*, toasted
(page 64)
4 cups (600 g) cooked
Sushi Rice (pages 12–13)
1 cup cooked lobster meat
$1/_2$ firm mango, sliced
3 tablespoons Homemade
Japanese Mayonnaise
(page 15)
1 tablespoon Thai chili sauce
$1/_2$ cup (25 g) mint leaves

1 Follow the directions for making California Rolls on page 55 using lobster meat, mango, mayonnaise, chili sauce and mint as the filling.

Makes 32 slices
Preparation time: **20 mins**
Assembling time: **30 mins**

Smoked Eel and Avocado California Rolls

1 whole ripe avocado, peeled and pitted
Juice from 1 lemon
3 sheets *nori*, toasted (page 64)
Small bowl of *tezu* (page 12)
3 cups (450 g) cooked Sushi Rice (pages 12–13)
$1/2$ cup *furikake* (topping for rice, see page 5)
$1/2$ lb (250 g) smoked conger eel (page 8), skinned
  and deboned or smoked trout or kippers

1 Slice the avocado lengthwise into $1/2$-in (1-cm) strips, place on a flat dish and drizzle with the lemon juice to prevent discoloring.
2 Place a bamboo mat in front of you, strips horizontal. Place 1 sheet of the *nori* on the mat, shiny side down with the edge of the *nori* $3/4$ in (2 cm) away from the edge of the mat closer to you.
3 To make the rolls, moisten hands with the *tezu* to prevent the rice from sticking. Spread 1 cup of the Sushi Rice evenly onto the *nori* with your fingers, leaving a $3/4$-in (2-cm) space at the top of the *nori*. Sprinkle the rice with some of the *furikake*.
4 Lay strips of the smoked eel and avocado down the middle of the rice.
5 Roll the mat as in the Maki Sushi (page 52). Shape the roll into a square and cut into 8 uniform slices. Repeat with the remaining *nori*, eel and avocado slices.

Makes 24 slices
Preparation time: **10 mins**

Inside-out California Rolls

1 red bell pepper
1 small zucchini, cut lengthwise into 8 strips
1 small, slender Japanese eggplant, halved lengthwise
   and cut into 1-in (2-cm) long slices
Olive oil for brushing
$1/_4$ teaspoon salt
$1/_4$ teaspoon freshly ground black pepper
2 sheets *nori*, toasted (page 64) and halved
3 cups (450 g) cooked Sushi Rice (pages 12–13)
$1/_2$ cup black sesame seeds
5 oz (150 g) mushrooms, sliced and sautéed in olive oil
2 tablespoons Coriander Pesto (page 15)

1 Preheat oven to 350°F (180°C/Gas mark 4). Bake the
bell pepper for 20 minutes or until the skin wrinkles.
Place it in a paper bag to steam and when the skin
loosens, run the pepper under cold water to peel the
skin off. Deseed and cut it into $1/_2$-in (1-cm)-long strips.
2 Brush the zucchini and eggplant lightly with the
olive oil. Sprinkle with the salt and pepper, and bake
until soft, about 5 minutes and set aside to cool.
3 Cover a sushi mat with a sheet of plastic wrap. Place
a half sheet of the *nori* on the mat. Spread $1/_3$ of the Sushi
Rice evenly over it. Sprinkle with some black sesame
seeds and cover with another layer of plastic wrap.
4 Place one hand between the first plastic sheet and the
bamboo mat. Place the other hand over the second plastic sheet. Turn the *nori* over so that the sesame seeds
are on the bottom and the *nori* is on top. Then, remove
the plastic wrap on the *nori*.
5 Layer the vegetables along the center of the *nori*. Spoon
a thin line of the Coriander Pesto close to the bell pepper.
6 Lift the front of the mat together with the sheet of
plastic wrap and roll up the sushi. When the front of
the mat is $3/_4$ in (2 cm) from the end of the sushi, lift
the mat and plastic wrap away from the sushi.
Continue rolling to complete the sushi roll.
7 Cut each roll into 8 uniform slices and serve.

Makes 24 slices
Cooking time: **20 mins**
Assembling time: **15 mins**

Inside-out Salmon Rolls

2 sheets *nori*, toasted (page 64)
9 thin slices smoked salmon (about 1 1/2 oz/50 g)
3 cups (450 g) cooked Sushi Rice (pages 12–13)
2 tablespoons toasted sesame seeds
1 Japanese cucumber, thinly sliced
3 tablespoons Pickled Ginger (page 40)

1 Using scissors, cut the *nori* into very thin, long strips.
2 Cover a bamboo mat with a sheet of plastic wrap.
Place 3 pieces of the smoked salmon on the mat, then
spread 1 cup of the Sushi Rice evenly over it. Sprinkle
with the toasted sesame seeds.
3 Cover the rice with a second sheet of plastic wrap.
Place one hand between the first plastic sheet and the
bamboo mat. Place the other hand over the second
plastic sheet. Turn it over so that the rice covered with
sesame seeds is facing the mat. Remove the plastic
wrap on the salmon.
4 Layer the prepared *nori*, cucumber and Pickled
Ginger down the center of the salmon.
5 Lift the front of the mat together with the plastic
wrap and roll up the sushi, applying even pressure.
When the front of the mat is $^3/_4$ in (2 cm) from the
end of the sushi, lift the mat and plastic wrap away
from the sushi. Continue rolling to complete the
sushi roll.
6 Cut each roll into 8 equal slices and serve with soy
sauce.

Makes 24 slices
Assembling time: **10 mins**

Hand-rolled Cone Sushi (Temaki Sushi)

3 sheets *nori*, toasted (see photo below)
Small bowl of *tezu* (page 12)
2 cups (300 g) cooked Sushi Rice (pages 12–13)
1 tablespoon wasabi paste
10 *shiso* leaves
1 Japanese cucumber, cut into 3-in (8-cm) lengths
5 oz (150 g) fresh salmon fillet, cut into 12 strips
1 Rolled Omelet (page 46), cut into 12 strips
2 oz (60 g) salmon roe
Pickled Ginger (page 40)
Soy Dipping Sauce (page 14)

1 After toasting the *nori* as shown below, cut it into 4 squares. Place 1 *nori* square diagonally in your left hand, shiny side facing down.

2 To make the rolls, moisten right hand with the *tezu* to prevent the rice from sticking. Place 2 tablespoons of the Sushi Rice on the *nori* square. Spread a dab of the wasabi paste on the rice, then a *shiso* leaf and top with the cucumber, salmon, omelet and salmon roe. Fold the edges of the *nori* towards the center to form a cone-shaped roll. Use a little water to seal the *nori*. Repeat with the remaining *nori* and all the other ingredients.

3 Serve with Pickled Ginger and Soy Dipping Sauce.

Serves 4
Preparation time: **15 mins**
Cooking time: **15 mins**

Toast the nori by holding it over a gas flame for about 30 seconds. It will change from black to a dark but bright green color.

Place the nori square diagonally in your left hand, shiny side facing down.

Place the various toppings over the rice on top of the nori.

Fold the edges of the nori in to form a cone-shaped roll.

Temaki Sushi with Garlic Ginger Chicken

2 tablespoons oil
2 large cloves garlic, crushed
1 in (2^1/$_2$ cm) fresh ginger, thinly sliced
2 small red chilies, deseeded and finely diced
^{1}/$_2$ cup water chestnuts, finely diced
7 oz (200 g) chicken breast, skin removed and cut into thin, long strips
1 teaspoon sake
1 teaspoon salt
^{1}/$_4$ teaspoon freshly ground black pepper
^{1}/$_4$ teaspoon fish sauce
^{1}/$_2$ teaspoon sesame oil
2 spring onions, sliced at an angle
3 sheets *nori*, toasted (page 64)
Small bowl of *tezu* (page 12)
2 cups (300 g) cooked Sushi Rice (pages 12–13)
Pickled Ginger (page 40)
Soy Dipping Sauce (page 14)

1 Heat the oil in a wok over medium heat and stir-fry the garlic, ginger and chilies for 5 seconds. Add the water chestnuts and chicken.

2 Toss the ingredients in the wok until the chicken is just cooked. Remove from the heat and drain. Place the cooked food into a bowl, season with sake, salt, pepper, fish sauce and sesame oil, and set aside to cool. When completely cold, stir in the spring onions and mix well.

3 Cut the *nori* sheets into 4 squares. Place 1 *nori* square diagonally in your left hand, shiny side facing down.

4 To make the rolls, moisten right hand with the *tezu* to prevent the rice from sticking. Place 2 tablespoons of the Sushi Rice on the *nori* square. Spoon 2 tablespoons of the chicken mixture on top of the rice and fold the edges of the *nori* in to form a cone-shaped roll. Use a little water to seal the *nori*. Repeat with the remaining ingredients.

5 Serve with Pickled Ginger and Soy Dipping Sauce.

Serves 4
Preparation time: **10 mins**
Cooking time: **20 mins**

Temaki Sushi with Asparagus and Smoked Trout

3 sheets *nori*, toasted (page 64)
1 smoked trout, skinned and deboned
1 tablespoon wasabi paste
$1/2$ cup (125 ml) Homemade Japanese Mayonnaise
  (page 15)
$1/4$ teaspoon salt
$1/4$ teaspoon freshly ground black pepper
6 stalks fresh asparagus, trimmed and cooked
Small bowl of *tezu* (page 12)
2 cups (300 g) cooked Sushi Rice (pages 12–13)
Soy Dipping Sauce (page 14)

1 Cut the toasted *nori* into 4 squares.
2 Combine the smoked trout, wasabi, mayonnaise, salt and black pepper in a mixing bowl.
3 Trim the asparagus spears into 3-in ($7^1/_2$-cm) lengths and cut in half crosswise to make 12 pieces.
4 Place a *nori* square diagonally in your left hand, shiny side facing down. To make the rolls, moisten right hand with the *tezu* to prevent the rice from sticking. Place 2 tablespoons of the Sushi Rice on the *nori* square. Put 1 piece of the asparagus down the center of the rice and add 2 tablespoons of the trout mixture. Fold the edges of the *nori* in to form a cone-shaped roll. Seal with a little water. Repeat with the remaining ingredients.
5 Serve with Soy Dipping Sauce.

Serves 4
Preparation time: **10 mins**
Assembling time: **20 mins**

Battleship Sushi
(Gunkan Sushi)

6 fresh scallops, cut into small cubes
2 tablespoons sake
1 spring onion, diced
Oil for grilling scallops
Small bowl of *tezu* (page 12)
2 cups (300 g) cooked Sushi Rice (pages 12–13)
4 sheets *nori*, toasted (page 64) and cut into 1-in
  (2$^1/_2$-cm) strips
4 oz (120 g) salmon or *tobiko* roe
4 oz (120 g) seasoned jellyfish (page 6), or fresh
  minced tuna
2 oz (60 g) seasoned *wakame* seaweed (page 9), or
  smoked oysters
3 oz (80 g) fresh clams

1 Marinate the scallops in the sake and spring onion
for 15 minutes. Remove scallops and drain.
2 Meanwhile, heat a grill and brush with the oil.
Cook the scallops for 2 minutes on both sides. Remove
from the heat and, when cool, cut the grilled scallops
into $^1/_2$-in (1-cm) cubes.
3 Moisten hands with the *tezu*. Take 1 tablespoon of
the Sushi Rice and form into an oval shape. Place the
rice oval on a flat surface and wrap a strip of the *nori*
around its sides, leaving the top and bottom uncov-
ered. The *nori* should be about $^1/_2$ in (1 cm) taller
than the rice it is wrapped around, and resemble a
battleship.
4 Continue shaping the remaining rice, wrapping
each rice oval with a strip of *nori*.
5 Spoon the cooked scallop onto 6 of the sushi.
Repeat with the salmon roe, jellyfish, seaweed and
clams to make 30 battleships in all.

Serves 4
Preparation time: **30 mins**
Assembling time: **30 mins**

Chicken Teriyaki Battleship Sushi

2 tablespoons soy sauce
2 tablespoons sake
1 teaspoon sugar
7 oz (200 g) chicken breast, skin removed and sliced into ³/₄-in (2-cm) strips
Small bowl of *tezu* (page 12)
2 cups (300 g) cooked Sushi Rice (pages 12–13)
4 sheets *nori*, toasted (page 64) and cut into 1-in (2¹/₂-cm) strips

1 Combine the soy sauce, sake and sugar in a small bowl and add the chicken strips. Marinate for 15 to 30 minutes. Drain the chicken.

2 Grill or broil the chicken over high heat for 1 minute on each side. Remove from the heat and leave to cool to room temperature.

3 Follow steps 3 through 5 for preparing Battleship Sushi on page 71.

4 When the chicken is cold, slice it very thin and arrange on top of the sushi to form battleships.

Serves 4
Preparation time: **30 mins**
Cooking time: **2 mins**
Assembling time: **15 mins**

Red Salmon Battleship Sushi

One 6-oz (185 g) can of good-quality salmon
3 tablespoons Homemade Japanese Mayonnaise (page 15)
$^1/_4$ teaspoon salt
$^1/_4$ teaspoon freshly ground black pepper
1 Japanese cucumber
Small bowl of *tezu* (page 12)
2 cups (300 g) cooked Sushi Rice (pages 12-13)
4 sheets *nori*, toasted (page 64) and cut into 1-in ($2^1/_2$-cm) strips

1 Drain the salmon and remove any skin and bones.
2 In a small bowl, mix the mayonnaise with the salmon, salt and black pepper. Do not overmix.
3 Slice the cucumber into very fine transparent circles. Place it on paper toweling and pat dry to remove excess moisture.
4 Follow steps 3 through 5 for preparing Battleship Sushi on page 71.
5 Spoon the salmon filling on the battleships. Top with the sliced cucumber to completely cover the fish.

Serves 4
Preparation time: **20 mins**
Assembling time: **15 mins**

Tuna with Daikon

8 oz (250 g) lean fresh tuna
1 tablespoon sesame paste (page 7)
1 cup (4 oz/125 g) daikon, sliced into matchsticks
Soy Dipping Sauce or Ponzu Sauce (pages 14–15)

Serves 2
Preparation time: **15 mins**

1 Slice the tuna to $^1/_8$-in (3-mm) thick. Cut each slice into strips $^3/_4$-in (2-cm) wide.

2 Spread the sesame paste on 1 side of each tuna strip.

3 To assemble, line up 1 tablespoon of the daikon evenly so that the sticks are parallel. Hold the daikon with the fingertips of one hand and wrap the tuna around the base of the daikon. The side of the tuna strip with sesame paste should face inside, touching the daikon. The tops of the daikon sticks should stand out slightly above the tuna wrap.

4 Stand the sashimi on a serving platter and serve with either Soy Dipping Sauce or Ponzu Sauce.

Squid with Nori

8 oz (250 g) squid, skinned, cleaned, and tentacles removed
2 sheets *nori*, toasted (page 64)
Soy Dipping Sauce or Ponzu Sauce (pages 14–15)

Serves 2
Preparation time: **15 mins**

1 Flatten the squid and insert the sharp point of a knife through the top of the sack, pulling the knife towards you to open the squid. Remove any fat and skin.

2 Cut the squid halves into six $2^1/_2$ x 3-in (6 x $7^1/_2$-cm) rectangles. Cut each rectangle into uniform strips, about 1 in ($2^1/_2$ cm) wide.

3 Using scissors, cut the *nori* into strips to exactly fit the squid strips.

4 Layer 3 strips of the squid alternating with 2 strips of the *nori*, beginning and ending with the squid. Cut the stack crosswise into 3 or 4 equal slices and serve with either Soy Dipping Sauce or Ponzu Sauce.

Salmon Rolls with Mayonnaise and Fish Roe

10 thin slices smoked salmon, about 2 oz (60 g)
2 cups (300 g) cooked Sushi Rice (pages 12–13)
3 tablespoons (45 ml) Homemade Japanese
  Mayonnaise (page 15)
1 teaspoon wasabi paste
2 tablespoons flying fish roe or caviar
2 tablespoons chives, thinly sliced

1 Cover a bamboo mat with plastic wrap. Place 5 pieces of the smoked salmon on the mat and spread 1 cup of the Sushi Rice on top. Dab half of the wasabi along the center of the rice.
2 Lift the front of the mat and roll the sushi, applying even pressure. When the front of the mat is $^3/_4$ in (2 cm) from the end of the sushi, pull the mat and plastic wrap away from the sushi. Continue rolling the sushi. The salmon should make a spiral effect through the rice.
3 Cut each roll into 8 uniform slices. Spoon $^1/_2$ teaspoon of the mayonnaise on top of each slice and garnish with the fish roe and chives.

Makes 16 slices
Preparation time: **10 mins**

Grilled Tofu with Vegetables

2 cakes (about 1 lb or 450 g) firm tofu, drained
4 fresh shiitake mushrooms, stems discarded
1 medium carrot, peeled and thinly sliced
1 medium potato, peeled and thinly sliced
1 green bell pepper, thinly sliced
1 small leek, rinsed and thinly sliced
1 egg white
1 teaspoon soy sauce
$1/4$ teaspoon salt
2 tablespoons sake
3 tablespoons cornstarch

1 Halve the tofu horizontally. Remove excess moisture by pressing it between sheets of paper toweling.
2 Cut the mushrooms into halves and slice thin.
3 Combine the mushrooms, carrot, potato, bell pepper, leek, egg white, soy sauce, salt and sake in a bowl. Sift 2 tablespoons of the cornstarch over the mixture and stir to mix well. Meanwhile, pre-heat the broiler.
4 Sift the remaining cornstarch over the tofu and pile the vegetable mixture on top. Using a spatula, lift the tofu and vegetables onto the broiler rack. Broil for 2 to 3 minutes or until the vegetables are lightly cooked.

Serves 4
Preparation time: **20 mins**
Cooking time: **5 mins**

Spinach with Sesame Seed Dressing

3 tablespoons white sesame seeds
$1/2$ teaspoon sugar
2 tablespoons soy sauce
3 tablespoons Basic Dashi Stock (page 16) or $1/4$ teaspoon instant *dashi* granules dissolved in 3 tablespoons boiling water
1 lb (450 g) fresh spinach, washed, stems discarded
1 teaspoon oil

Serves 4
Preparation time: **10 mins**
Cooking time: **5 mins**

1 Dry-roast (without using oil) the sesame seeds in a large skillet over medium to low heat until golden brown, about 3 minutes. Set aside 1 teaspoon of the toasted sesame seeds to use as a garnish. Using a mortar and pestle, grind the remaining seeds until smooth.
2 Blend the sugar, soy sauce and *dashi* stock with the sesame seed paste to make a dressing. Set aside.
3 Drain excess water from the spinach. Heat the oil in a medium saucepan over high heat and add a handful of the spinach leaves, stirring with a wooden spoon until the leaves have wilted. Continue stirring, adding more spinach as each batch cooks down. Do not overcook.
4 Place the cooked spinach in a colander and squeeze out excess moisture with the back of a wooden spoon. Combine the spinach and dressing in a small bowl. Transfer to a platter and garnish with the reserved sesame seeds. Serve hot or at room temperature.

Bean Sprouts and Bell Pepper Salad

8 oz (3 cups/250 g) bean sprouts, trimmed
1 large carrot, peeled and thinly sliced
1 large green bell pepper, thinly sliced
2 teaspoons toasted sesame seeds, to garnish

Dressing
3 tablespoons soy sauce
2 tablespoons rice vinegar
1 tablespoon oil
1 teaspoon sesame oil

1 Wash the bean sprouts in cold water and drain well.
2 Make the Dressing in a small bowl.
3 Blanch the carrot in a saucepan with well-salted boiling water, for 30 seconds. Add the bean sprouts and bell pepper and blanch for another 30 seconds. Drain and plunge the vegetables into a pan of ice water. When cool, drain well in a colander and set aside.
4 Just before serving, place the cooled vegetables in a serving bowl. Dress and toss the vegetables well. Distribute the salad into 4 individual serving bowls, garnish with the sesame seeds, and serve.

Serves 4
Preparation time: **20 mins**
Cooking time: **3 mins**

Savory Japanese Pumpkin

1 lb (450 g) pumpkin or
butternut squash
2 cups (500 ml) Basic
Dashi Stock (page 16)
or 1 teaspoon instant
dashi granules dissolved
in 2 cups (500 ml)
boiling water
2 tablespoons sugar
1 tablespoon *mirin*
2 tablespoons soy sauce

Serves 4
Preparation time: **10 mins**
Cooking time: **20 mins**

1 Cut the pumpkin into 2-in (5-cm) square chunks, leaving the skin on.

2 Using the sharp point of a knife, cut away small pieces of the pumpkin skin to give a mottled effect. Place the pumpkin, skin side down in a saucepan with a heavy base.

3 Add $1^1/_2$ cups of the *dashi* stock, sugar and *mirin* and cover the saucepan.

4 Bring to a slow boil over medium heat and simmer for about 8 minutes, turning the pumpkin over after 4 minutes.

5 Add the soy sauce and the remaining *dashi* stock.

6 Cook, covered, until the pumpkin is tender. Serve immediately or let it cool to room temperature. The broth is delicious over rice.

Wakame and Tuna with Soy Dressing

2 sheets (10 g) *wakame* (page 9)
2 cups (500 ml) water
Two 6-oz (170-g) cans of water-packed tuna
2 teaspoons lemon juice
1 Japanese cucumber, thinly sliced
1 tomato, diced

Dressing
3 tablespoons rice vinegar
2 tablespoons soy sauce
1 teaspoon sugar
2 teaspoons sesame oil

Serves 4
Preparation time: **30 mins**
Assembling time: **3 mins**

1 Soak the dried *wakame* in a bowl of cold water to soften, about 20 minutes.

2 To make the Dressing, combine the vinegar, soy sauce, sugar and oil in a small bowl, stirring until the sugar is dissolved.

3 Bring the water to a boil in a small saucepan. Blanch the *wakame* for 30 seconds, drain and rinse under cold water. Pat dry with paper toweling. Remove any hard veins from the *wakame* and slice it into $1/2$-in (1-cm) strips.

4 Drain the tuna and place it in a mixing bowl. Sprinkle with the lemon juice and use a fork to break the tuna into bite-sized pieces.

5 Combine the *wakame*, cucumber and tomato with the tuna and toss with the Dressing. Serve immediately.

Eggplant Stir-fried with Ginger and Miso

$^1/_2$ cup (125 ml) water
$^1/_4$ cup (60 ml) miso
2 tablespoons soy sauce
2 tablespoons sugar
3 tablespoons oil
1 tablespoon fresh
  ginger, finely diced
1 lb (450 g) slender
  Japanese eggplant, cut
  into chunks
1 large red or green bell
  pepper, cut into chunks
2 tablespoons sake
2 teaspoons cornstarch,
  mixed with a little
  water to make a paste

1 Combine the water, miso, soy sauce and sugar in a small bowl, and stir until the sugar is dissolved. Set aside.

2 Heat the oil in a wok over high heat. Stir-fry the ginger, eggplant and bell pepper until the vegetables are almost tender, about 3 minutes.

3 Add the sake and stir-fry for another 20 seconds. Then add the miso mixture.

4 Stir in the cornstarch paste and continue stir-frying until the sauce thickens. Serve immediately.

Serves 4
Preparation time: **10 mins**
Cooking time: **5 mins**

Tofu and Udon Noodles in Clear Soup

4 slices deep-fried tofu,
(*abura-age*, see page 9)
8 cups (2 liters) water
12 oz (400 g) dried udon
noodles
6 cups (1 1/2 liters) Basic
Dashi Stock (page 16)
or 1 tablespoon instant
dashi granules dis-
solved in 6 cups (1 1/2
liters) boiling water
2 tablespoons sugar
6 tablespoons soy sauce
3 tablespoons *mirin*
1/2 teaspoon salt
1 small leek, rinsed and
thinly sliced
Seven-spice chili mix,
to garnish

Serves 4
Preparation time: **10 mins**
Cooking time: **20 mins**

1 Rinse the deep-fried tofu slices under boiling water to remove excess oil. Drain and pat dry with paper toweling. Cut each slice of tofu into quarters to yield 16 pieces.

2 Bring the water to a boil and add the noodles, stirring gently to keep them separate. Cook at a vigorous boil for 5 minutes or until the noodles are cooked but still firm. Drain in a colander and refresh under cold water. Drain again and cover with a damp kitchen towel until completely cool.

3 Place 1 cup of the *dashi* stock, sugar and tofu in a saucepan and bring to a boil. Just before boiling, reduce heat to low and cook for another 2 minutes. Add 2 tablespoons of the soy sauce and simmer until almost all the liquid has evaporated. Remove from the heat.

4 Heat the remaining *dashi* stock, soy sauce, *mirin* and salt in a saucepan over high heat. When it is just about to boil, add the leek and remove from the heat.

5 Distribute the noodles into 4 individual serving bowls. Top with the tofu and ladle the broth over it ensuring that each bowl has some leek. Garnish with the chili mix and serve immediately.

Cold Soba Noodles (Zaru Soba)

8 cups (2 liters) water
10 oz (300 g) dried soba
noodles
1$^1/_3$ cups (350 ml) Basic
Dashi Stock (page 16)
or $^3/_4$ teaspoon instant
dashi granules dis-
solved in 1$^1/_3$ cups
(350 ml) boiling water
5 tablespoons soy sauce
3 tablespoons *mirin*
1 tablespoon sugar
1 sheet *nori*, toasted
(page 64) and cut into
thin strips
4 teaspoons wasabi
paste
2 spring onions, thinly
sliced

1 Bring the water to a boil in a large saucepan over high heat and add the noodles, stirring gently to keep them separate. Cook at a vigorous boil until the noodles are cooked but still firm, about 5 minutes. Drain in a colander and rinse under cold water. Drain the noodles again and cover with a damp cloth until completely cool.
2 Heat the *dashi* stock, soy sauce, *mirin* and sugar in a small saucepan and cook over medium heat until the sugar is dissolved. Just before boiling, remove from the heat and set aside.
3 Distribute the cold noodles into 4 individual serving bowls and top each bowl with a quarter of the *nori*.
4 Pour the dipping sauce into 4 small bowls and stir in some of the wasabi and spring onions. Dip the noodles into the sauce before eating.

Serves 4
Preparation time: **10 mins**
Cooking time: **15 mins**

Chilled Noodles with Shrimp and Tomato

1 1/2 cups (375 ml) Basic Dashi Stock (page 16) or 3/4 teaspoon instant *dashi* granules dissolved in 1 1/2 cups (375 ml) boiling water
1/3 cup (90 ml) *mirin*
1/3 cup (90 ml) soy sauce
10 cups (2 1/2 liters) water
8 oz (250 g) dried *somen* noodles
12 medium shrimp, peeled and deveined
Ice water plus ice cubes
2 medium ripe tomatoes, each cut into 6 wedges
1 Japanese cucumber, thinly sliced diagonally
2 spring onions, sliced
2 tablespoons freshly grated ginger

1 To make the sauce, combine the *dashi* stock, *mirin* and soy sauce and cook until just boiling. Set aside.
2 Bring 8 cups of water to a boil in a large saucepan and add the noodles, stirring gently to keep them separate. Cook at a vigorous boil until the noodles are cooked but still firm, about 5 minutes. Drain in a colander and rinse under cold water. Drain again and cover with a damp cloth until completely cool.
3 Bring 2 cups of salted water to a boil in a saucepan, and poach the shrimp until they turn pink and opaque, about 1 minute. Drain and cool.
4 Distribute the noodles into 4 serving bowls and cover with ice water. Add 3 ice cubes to each bowl and arrange the shrimp, tomato and cucumber on top.
5 Place the spring onions and ginger into 4 small dishes and pour the sauce over it. Dip the noodles, shrimp and vegetables into the sauce before eating.

Serves 4
Preparation time: **30 mins**   Cooking time: **5 mins**

Japanese-style Plain Steamed Rice

3 cups (600 g) uncooked short-grain Japanese rice
3 cups (750 ml) water

Serves 4–6
Preparation time: **5 mins**
Cooking time: **35 mins**

1 Cover the uncooked rice in cold water and wash it thoroughly by rubbing the grains between your hands until the water is quite cloudy. Drain and repeat several times until the water rinses off clear.
2 Place the rice in a saucepan with a heavy base. Fill with the water, cover with a lid and bring to a boil.
3 When it starts to boil, lower the heat and simmer the rice for 20 minutes. By this time, most of the water would have been absorbed. Remove the saucepan from the heat and leave the rice to stand for 10 minutes with the lid on.
4 Using a wet rice paddle (*shamoji*, page 4) or a fork, fluff up the rice and serve in heated individual rice bowls.

Rice with Three Toppings

2 cups (400 g) uncooked short-grain Japanese rice
2 cups (500 ml) water
2 tablespoons sugar
2 tablespoons soy sauce
2 tablespoons sake
1 tablespoon fresh ginger juice
8 oz (250 g) ground chicken
2 cups fresh or frozen peas
8 large eggs, beaten
$1/_2$ teaspoon salt
Pickled Ginger (page 40), to garnish

Serves 4
Preparation time: **15 mins**
Cooking time: **35 mins**

1 Cook the rice (see instructions above), but keep the rice warm in a covered saucepan until needed.
2 Combine 1 tablespoon of the sugar, 1 tablespoon of the soy sauce, 1 tablespoon of the sake, and the ginger juice in a saucepan. Bring to a boil and add the chicken, stirring with a wooden spoon to break up the clumps. Cook for about 3 minutes. Remove from the heat and set aside.
3 Cook the peas in boiling water until tender, about 4 minutes. Drain and set aside.
4 Place the eggs, salt and the remaining sugar, soy sauce and sake in a saucepan. Cook over low heat, stirring constantly, until the eggs are set but still moist, about 4 minutes. Remove from the heat.
5 Spoon the cooked rice into 4 individual bowls and place equal amounts of the 3 toppings over the rice in distinct sections. Garnish with Pickled Ginger and serve immediately.

Mixed Vegetables on Sushi Rice

Kanpyo

1 oz (30 g) dried gourd strips (*kanpyo*)
1 cup (250 ml) Basic Dashi Stock (page 16) or $^1/_2$ teaspoon instant *dashi* granules dissolved in 1 cup (250 ml) boiling water
2 tablespoons soy sauce
1 tablespoon *mirin*

Sushi

6 dried or fresh shiitake mushrooms
2 slices deep-fried tofu (*abura-age*, see page 9)
1 section (4 oz/125 g) fresh lotus root, peeled
1 teaspoon vinegar
1 medium carrot
$^1/_2$ cup (125 ml) Basic Dashi Stock (page 16) or $^1/_4$ teaspoon instant *dashi* granules dissolved in $^1/_2$ cup (125 ml) boiling water
1$^1/_2$ tablespoons sugar
$^1/_2$ teaspoon salt
1$^1/_2$ tablespoons soy sauce
1 tablespoon *mirin*
5 cups (750 g) cooked Sushi Rice (pages 12–13)

Garnish

1 Sesame Omelet (page 30), cut in strips
2 oz (60 g) snow peas, thinly sliced
$^1/_2$ sheet *nori*, toasted (page 64) and shredded
Pickled Ginger (page 40)

1 If using dried mushrooms, soften them in hot water, about 20 minutes.

2 Rinse the dried gourd in cold water. Mix the gourd with a little salt and rub it between your hands to soften, and rinse in cold water again. Place the gourd in a saucepan and cover with cold water. Bring to a boil over medium-high heat and cook for 10 minutes. Drain.

3 Place the *dashi* stock, soy sauce, sugar, *mirin* and the gourd into a saucepan and bring to a boil over medium to high heat. Reduce heat to low and cook until the gourd is tender and slightly translucent, about 20 minutes. Most of the liquid will be absorbed. Drain and set aside. When cool enough to handle, cut the gourd into $^3/_4$-in (2-cm) pieces.

4 Drain the mushrooms and squeeze out excess moisture, reserving $^1/_2$ cup (125 ml) of the liquid. Discard the stems and slice the mushroom caps thinly.

5 Rinse the tofu slices in boiling water in a colander to remove excess oil. Drain, then pat dry with paper toweling. Cut each piece lengthwise in half, then slice each half into thin strips.

6 Cut the lotus root into thin slices. If the root is large, cut the slices into $^3/_4$-in (2-cm) strips. Soak strips in 1 cup of water mixed with the vinegar for 5 minutes. Drain and set aside.

7 Cut the carrot lengthwise into quarters. Cut each quarter into 1-in (2$^1/_2$-cm) pieces. Turn the flat side of the carrot onto a board and cut into very thin slices.

8 Heat the reserved mushroom liquid with the *dashi* stock, sugar, salt, soy sauce and *mirin*. Add mushrooms, tofu, lotus root and carrot, and cook until tender, about 10 minutes. Remove from the heat and drain.

9 To assemble and serve, carefully stir the gourd and vegetables with the Sushi Rice. Do not overmix. Place the rice mixture into individual serving bowls and arrange small amounts of each garnish on top.

Serves 4
Preparation time: **45 mins**
Cooking time: **10 mins**

Azuki Bean Rice

3/4 cup (150 g) dried red beans (*azuki*, page 7), washed and drained
3 1/2 cups (750 g) uncooked glutinous rice (page 6), washed and drained
1/4 teaspoon Sesame Salt (page 15)

Serves 4 to 6
Preparation time: 45 mins
  + overnight soaking
Cooking time: 35–50 mins

1 Place the red beans in a saucepan and cover with water. Bring to a boil and drain the beans, refresh in cold water, and bring to a boil again.
2 Reduce the heat to low, cover and simmer until the beans are tender, about 40 minutes, adding more water as needed to keep beans covered.
3 Drain the beans, reserving the liquid. Pour the reserved liquid from the beans onto the uncooked rice grains and let is stand, covered, overnight to allow the rice to take on a pinkish color.
4 Drain the rice and reserve the liquid. Combine the beans and rice, taking care not to crush the beans. Bring water to a boil in the base of a steamer. Line the steamer with cheesecloth and spread the rice and beans mixture on it. Poke a few holes in the rice for the steam to escape.
5 Steam over high heat until the rice is cooked, about 50 minutes, basting frequently with the reserved red bean liquid.
6 Serve the rice and beans mixture in individual heated serving bowls and sprinkle with the Sesame Salt. This dish can also be served at room temperature.

Tempura

$^1/_2$ cup (60 g) all-purpose flour for dredging
1 Japanese eggplant, cut diagonally into long, thick slices
3 cups (4 oz/120 g) pumpkin or sweet potato, peeled and sliced
12 green beans (4 oz/125 g), trimmed
1 small onion, cut in crescents
4 fresh shiitake mushrooms, stems discarded
$^2/_3$ cup (90 g) fresh or frozen green peas
8 medium shrimp, peeled and deveined, tails intact
4 whitebait, about 2 oz (60 g) each or white fish fillets, sliced
4 scallops, cleaned and sliced in half horizontally
Oil for deep-frying
Tempura Dipping Sauce (page 14)

Batter
2 egg yolks
2 cups (500 ml) ice water
2 cups (250 g) all-purpose flour

Serves 4
Preparation time: **20 mins**
Cooking time: **30 mins**

1 Put the flour for dredging in a mixing bowl and set aside.
2 Heat the oil in a wok or deep-fryer to 325°F (160°C).
3 To prepare the first batch of Batter, beat 1 of the egg yolk with 1 cup of the ice water in a mixing bowl until smooth. Add 1 cup of the flour, all at once, and stir briefly with a fork or chopsticks until just combined. The Batter may be lumpy but it should be quite thin. Do not overmix.
4 Dredge the eggplant, pumpkin, green beans and onion pieces in the flour and shake off any excess. Dip a slice of the vegetable into the Batter and gently shake off any excess.
5 Carefully slip the vegetables, 5 to 6 pieces at a time, into the hot oil and cook, turning once until crisp, about 2 to 3 minutes. Remove the fried vegetables from the oil with a slotted spoon and drain on a wire rack or paper toweling.
6 To cook the mushrooms, spoon the Batter on the underside of the mushrooms, shaking off any excess. Place the mushrooms in oil, batter side down and fry, turning once until tender, about 1 minute. Remove the fried mushroom from the oil with a slotted spoon and drain on paper toweling.
7 Sprinkle the green peas lightly with the flour. Scoop about 1 tablespoon of the peas onto a slotted spoon and coat the peas in the Batter. Let excess Batter from the peas drip from the spoon. Carefully place the peas into the oil and cook for 2 to 3 minutes, turning once, until the Batter is crisp. Remove the fried peas from the oil and drain on paper toweling.
8 Heat oil to 350°F (180°C) and prepare the second batch of the Batter. Dredge the seafood with the flour and dip into the Batter. Cook the seafood until golden and crisp, about 3 minutes (Shrimp may take 1 minute more, depending on the size). Remove the fried seafood from the oil with a slotted spoon and drain on paper toweling.
9 Pour about 3 tablespoons of the warm Tempura Dipping Sauce into small sauce bowls and serve with the selection of tempura.

Salmon Teriyaki

1 lb (450 g) fresh salmon fillet, quartered
2 tablespoons soy sauce
1 tablespoon *mirin*
2 teaspoons sake
1 tablespoon oil
1 cup (2 oz/90 g) daikon, peeled and grated

1 Place the salmon fillets in a large baking pan.
Combine the soy sauce, *mirin* and sake in a small
bowl and pour it over the salmon pieces to marinate
for 10 minutes. Drain the salmon and reserve the
marinade.
2 Heat the broiler and brush the rack lightly with the
oil. Place the fish on the rack, skin side up, and brush
it lightly with the reserved marinade. Grill the fish
until the skin is lightly browned and crispy, about 4
minutes.
3 Turn the salmon pieces over and brush again lightly
with the marinade. Grill until the salmon is just cooked
through and the flesh flakes easily with a fork, about 4
minutes.
4 Transfer the grilled fish to serving plates and spoon
the remaining marinade over it. Serve immediately
with the grated daikon and rice.

For equally delicious **Scallop Teriyaki**, substitute with
1 lb (450 g) trimmed large scallops. For **Grilled
Teriyaki Vegetables**, use assorted vegetables such as
asparagus, eggplant, red bell peppers and
shiitake mushrooms.

Serves 4
Preparation time: **15 mins**
Cooking time: **10 mins**

Baked Fish with Vegetables

2 tablespoons sake
1 teaspoon soy sauce
1 teaspoon fresh ginger juice
1 teaspoon salt
1 $1/_2$ lbs (675 g) white fish fillets (such as flounder,
  sole, sea bass or cod), cut in 4 equal pieces
4 pieces aluminum foil, each 10-in (25-cm) square
1 tablespoon oil
1 large carrot, peeled and thinly sliced
1 medium onion, peeled and thinly sliced
1 medium bell pepper, deseeded and thinly sliced
$1/_2$ lemon, sliced

1 Combine the sake, soy sauce, ginger juice and salt in
a shallow baking dish. Coat the fish well with this
mixture and set aside to marinate for 10 minutes.
Drain, reserving the marinade.
2 Heat oven to 325°F (160°C/Gas mark 3). Place one
fillet in the center of each of the aluminum foil,
brush with the oil, and sprinkle with the carrot,
onion, bell pepper and reserved marinade. To seal the
packet, bring the two sides of the foil over the fish
and crimp closed. Fold up each end of the foil and
place each packet on a baking sheet.
3 Bake for about 20 minutes or until the fish flakes
easily with a fork. Place the packets on a serving plate
or carefully transfer the fish and vegetables from the
foil to a serving plate, pouring any remaining juices
over it. Garnish with the lemon slices and serve.

Serves 4
Preparation time: **15 mins**
Cooking time: **20 mins**

Marinated Deep-fried Baby Octopus

2 lbs (1 kg) fresh baby octopus or squid
$1/2$ cup (120 ml) sake
2 tablespoons soy sauce
$1/2$ cup (60 g) all-purpose flour
Oil for deep-frying
4 lemon or lime wedges, to garnish

Sauce
4 tablespoons Worcestershire sauce
4 tablespoons tomato ketchup
2 tablespoons lemon juice

1 Clean the baby octopus or squid by peeling the outer layer of skin under cold running water.
2 Combine the sake and soy sauce in a bowl and coat the octopus in the mixture. Set aside to marinate in a cool place for 2 hours or overnight in the refrigerator.
3 To make the Sauce, combine the Worcestershire sauce, tomato ketchup and lemon juice in a small serving bowl and set aside.
4 Drain the octopus and dredge each piece in the flour.
5 Heat the oil to 325°F (160°C) and cook 4 to 6 pieces of the octopus at a time for about 2 minutes, or until crispy. Drain on a wire rack and repeat until all the octopus is cooked.
6 Serve immediately with the Sauce and lemon wedges.

Serves 4
Preparation time: **15 mins**
Cooking time: **10 mins**

Braised Flounder (Karei Nitsuka)

4 whole flounders, about
8 oz (225 g) each,
cleaned
3 cups (750 ml) water
1 teaspoon salt
$^1/_2$ cup (125 ml) sake
$^1/_2$ cup (125 ml) soy
sauce
2 tablespoons *mirin*
3 tablespoons sugar
1 in (2$^1/_2$ cm) fresh
ginger, thinly sliced
2 cups (125 g) fresh
spinach, washed,
trimmed, tied in small
parcels

Serves 4
Preparation time: **20 mins**
Cooking time: **10 mins**

1 Using a sharp knife, score each fish on one side by making 2 parallel diagonal incisions about 1$^1/_4$ in (3 cm) apart. Turn the fish over and make 2 more parallel incisions on the diagonal. Make the cuts deep enough to almost touch the bone.

2 Combine the water, salt, sake, soy sauce, *mirin* and sugar and bring to a boil in a deep skillet. Add the fresh ginger and cook for another 30 seconds.

3 Place the fish in a single layer in the skillet, overlapping heads and tails as necessary. When the liquid returns to a boil, reduce the heat to low and simmer the fish for 2 minutes.

4 Spoon the liquid over the fish periodically but do not turn the fish over. Simmer for another 3 minutes, continually basting, until the fish flakes easily with a fork.

5 Place the spinach parcels alongside the fish and cook for 30 seconds. Remove from the heat.

6 Carefully lift the fish and spinach onto serving plates and spoon some of the cooking liquid over it. Serve immediately with steamed rice.

Seafood and Chicken Hotpot

8 fresh or dried shiitake mushrooms, stems discarded, tops scored crosswise

1 carrot, thinly sliced

6 mussels or large clams

2 tablespoons plus ¹/₂ teaspoon salt

8 oz (225 g) *shirataki* or glass noodles

6 cups (1¹/₂ liters) Basic Dashi Stock (page 16) or 1 tablespoon instant *dashi* granules dissolved in 6 cups (1¹/₂ liters) boiling water

1 tablespoon *mirin*

1 tablespoon soy sauce

¹/₂ teaspoon salt

8 oz (225 g) chicken breast

8 oz (225 g) fish fillets, such as sea bass, mackerel, or salmon, cubed

4 large scallops

6 oz (180 g) shucked oysters

8 medium shrimp, peeled and deveined, tails intact

4 leaves Chinese or Napa cabbage, cut in 2-in (5-cm) squares

1 large or 2 small leeks

10 oz (300 g) firm tofu

Pinch of chili pepper

1 cup (250 ml) Ponzu Sauce (page 15)

6 tablespoons daikon, grated

1 spring onion, thinly sliced

1 If using dried mushrooms, soften in hot water for 20 minutes and drain. Blanch the carrot and set aside. Soak the mussels or clams for 5 minutes in 4 cups of cold water mixed with 2 tablespoons of salt. Rinse the seafood under cold running water and drain. Blanch the *shirataki* noodles for 2 minutes, drain and when cool enough to handle, cut into 4-in (10-cm) lengths. Place the mushrooms, carrot, mussels and noodles into a deep saucepan.

2 Pour the *dashi* stock, *mirin*, soy sauce and salt into the saucepan and bring to a slow boil. Pour enough liquid over the ingredients in the dish to almost cover it and let it simmer over low heat. Do not boil.

3 Remove the skin on the chicken and cut the meat into cubes. Rinse the leeks clean. Arrange the ingredients into 4 small batches—chicken, seafood, vegetables and tofu—in a hotpot on a table-top hotplate and cook them in batches. Add the chili pepper, if desired.

4 As the ingredients continue to cook, diners can help themselves from the cookpot. Serve with individual dipping bowls of the Ponzu Sauce stirred with the daikon and spring onion. Replenish the hotpot with the remaining ingredients and the *dashi* stock as needed.

Serves 4 to 6
Preparation time: **30 mins**
Cooking time: **20 mins**

Yakitori (Grilled Skewered Chicken)

1 tablespoon sugar
$^1/_4$ cup (60 ml) *mirin*
$^1/_2$ cup (125 ml) soy sauce
$^1/_2$ cup (125 ml) sake
1 lb (450 g) boneless chicken
7 oz (200 g) chicken livers
4 fresh shiitake mushrooms, stems discarded
1 leek, cut into pieces
2 green bell peppers, cut into squares
16 to 20 skewers, 8 in (20 cm) long
Seven-spice chili mix
Lemon wedges, to garnish

1 To prepare the sauce, combine the sugar, *mirin*, soy sauce and sake in a saucepan and bring to a boil. Reduce the heat to low and simmer for 15 minutes, reducing the sauce to 1 cup.

2 Cut the chicken and liver into cubes, then thread them through the skewers, alternating with pieces of the mushroom, leek and bell pepper. If bamboo skewers are used, soak them in water for at least 10 minutes prior to use.

3 Heat the grill. Baste the ingredients with the sauce.

4 Grill the prepared food for 2 to 3 minutes, turning 3 or 4 times and basting each time, until the chicken and livers are just cooked. Do not overcook.

5 Remove the skewers from the heat. Sprinkle the grilled food with chili mix and serve with lemon wedges.

Serves 4
Preparation time: **30 mins**
Cooking time: **5 mins**

Crispy Chicken Chunks

2 teaspoons fresh ginger
  juice
1 clove garlic, thinly
  sliced
1 tablespoon soy sauce
1 tablespoon sake
1 lb (450 g) boneless
  chicken, cut into chunks
2/3 cup (90 g) cornstarch
3 cups (750 g) oil for
  deep-frying
Lemon wedges, to
  garnish
Mustard Sauce (page 14)

Serves 4
Preparation time: **30 mins**
Cooking time: **10 mins**

1 Combine the ginger juice, garlic, soy sauce and sake in a mixing bowl. Marinate the chicken pieces in the soy mixture for 20 minutes.
2 Drain the chicken and toss it lightly in cornstarch, shaking off any excess.
3 Meanwhile, heat the oil to 325°F (160°C). Fry the chicken, about 4 to 5 pieces at a time, until golden and cooked through, about 4 minutes.
4 Remove the chicken from the oil with a slotted spoon and drain on paper toweling. When the oil returns to 325°F (160°C), add more of the chicken pieces and repeat until all the chicken is cooked. Keep the cooked chicken warm until serving. Arrange on individual serving plates and garnish with lemon wedges. Serve with the Mustard Sauce.

Stir-fried Tofu with Chicken, Egg and Vegetables

4 dried or fresh shiitake mushrooms, stems discarded
10 oz (300 g) firm tofu
1 tablespoon oil
8 oz (250 g) ground chicken
1 tablespoon (1 in/2$^1/_2$ cm) freshly grated ginger
3 tablespoons sake
1 carrot, shaved into thin, wide strips
1 tablespoon sugar
2 tablespoons soy sauce
1 large egg, beaten
4 spring onions, cut in $^1/_2$-in (1-cm) lengths

1 If using dried mushrooms, soak them in hot water until soft, about 20 minutes. Drain the mushrooms and squeeze out any excess water. Slice caps thinly crosswise.
2 Break the tofu coarsely with a fork and set aside to drain.
3 Heat the oil in a saucepan over medium to high heat, and stir-fry the chicken for 2 minutes, breaking it into small pieces with a wooden spoon.
4 Add the ginger and mushrooms and cook for another 2 minutes.
5 Add the sake and carrots and stir-fry over high heat, for 1 minute.
6 Reduce heat to medium and add the tofu. Stir-fry for 1 minute until heated through.
7 Dissolve the sugar in the soy sauce in a small bowl and add to the beaten egg. Add the egg mixture into the saucepan and stir until just cooked, about 2 minutes. Fold in the spring onions and serve immediately.

Serves 4
Preparation time: **10 mins**
Cooking time: **10 mins**

Sesame Chicken Loaf

1 lb (450 g) ground chicken
1 small leek, finely diced
1 tablespoon freshly grated ginger
1 tablespoon soy sauce
1 tablespoon sake
1 egg, beaten
1 tablespoon oil
2 tablespoons toasted sesame seeds
Mustard Sauce (page 14)

Serves 4 to 6
Preparation time: **15 mins**
Cooking time: **10 mins**

1 Combine the chicken, leek, ginger, soy sauce, sake and egg in a bowl and mix well.

2 Heat the oil in a small skillet, and spread the chicken mixture evenly to cover the bottom of the pan. Cook over medium heat for 2 to 3 minutes, or until the underside of the mixture is brown. Cut the chicken mixture into quarters, and turn the wedges over to cook for another 2 to 3 minutes.

3 Transfer the chicken wedges to a chopping board and slice into smaller pieces for serving. Sprinkle with the toasted sesame seeds and serve with the Mustard Sauce.

Mix the chicken, leek, ginger, soy sauce, sake and egg in a bowl until well combined.

Spread the chicken mixture evenly over the base of the pan and brown the underside.

Cut the loaf into quarters, then turn the wedges over to cook the other side.

Slice the chicken wedges into smaller serving portions on a chopping board.

Chicken Hotpot (Mitzutaki)

2 tablespoons uncooked rice
2 lbs (1 kg) chicken, cut into 2-in (5-cm) chunks
4-in (10-cm) piece *konbu*, wiped clean and cut into 4 strips
1 tablespoon sake
1 teaspoon salt
1 teaspoon sugar
8 cups (2 liters) water
2 cups Ponzu Sauce (page 15)
¹/₂ cup daikon, grated
Pinch of chili pepper
4 leaves Chinese or Napa cabbage, cut in squares
8 fresh shiitake mushrooms, stems discarded and tops scored
2 small leeks, rinsed and sliced diagonally
1 carrot, peeled and thinly sliced
8 oz (250 g) *shirataki* or glass noodles
10 oz (300 g) soft tofu, cubed
Seven-spice chili mix or *sansho* pepper (page 7)
Lime or lemon wedges
2 cups fresh udon noodles (optional)

1 Wrap the rice in a 4-in (10-cm) square piece muslin or cheesecloth and secure with a string.

2 Place the rice bag, chicken, *konbu*, sake, salt, sugar and water in a large saucepan and bring to a boil. Just before it boils, remove and discard the *konbu*. Reduce heat to low and simmer for about 20 minutes, occasionally skimming the surface to remove foam or debris.

3 Meanwhile, divide the Ponzu Sauce into 4 small serving bowls. Mix the daikon and chili pepper together and place in small bowl as a garnish. Arrange the prepared vegetables, *shirataki* noodles and tofu on a serving platter.

4 Remove the rice parcels from the broth. Strain and reserve the broth. Transfer the chicken to a hotpot on a table-top hotplate and pour the reserved broth over it.

5 At the table, bring the chicken and broth to a boil. Arrange the ingredients in 4 batches—vegetables, *shirataki* noodles and tofu—into a hotpot on a table-top hotplate. When the ingredients in the hotpot are cooked, diners can help themselves to the food.

6 Replenish the hotpot with the remaining ingredients as necessary. Serve with seven-spice chili mix, daikon-chili mixture and lime wedges. When all the ingredients are used up, cook the udon noodles in the simmering liquid for 3 minutes. Ladle the noodles into individual serving bowls and serve.

Serves 4
Preparation time: **30 mins**
Cooking time: **40 mins**

Japanese Mixed Grill

For a successful grill, combine various types of meat—chicken, beef or pork tenderloin, boneless lamb, calf and chicken liver—with seafood and vegetables.

4 large mussels, scrubbed and beards removed
1 lb (450 g) lean boneless beef, pork, or lamb, cut into cubes
8 jumbo shrimp, peeled and deveined, tails intact
8 fresh shiitake mushrooms, stems discarded
2 bell peppers, deseeded and cut lengthwise into long strips
2 small leeks, rinsed and sliced
1 medium onion, peeled and cut in wedges
1 large carrot, peeled and sliced
1 large sweet potato, peeled and sliced
2 ears of corn, husked and quartered
1 eggplant, sliced
1 tablespoon oil
Sesame Seed Sauce (page 14)
Ponzu Sauce (page 15)
$1/_2$ cup daikon, grated
2 spring onions, thinly sliced
4 tablespoons seven-spice chili mix
$1/_4$ cup (60 ml) prepared Japanese mustard

1 Arrange the ingredients in 4 small batches on a serving platter, grouping the meats and vegetables together.
2 At the table, brush the oil onto a flat, heatproof table-top grill over medium heat and add about a quarter of each of the ingredients from the platter. Cook until done to taste, 4 to 6 minutes, turning occasionally. Diners may use chopsticks to remove the cooked meat or vegetables from the table-top vessel.
3 Replenish with the remaining ingredients as needed. Serve with a choice of the Sesame Seed Sauce, Ponzu Sauce, daikon, spring onions, chili mix and mustard.

Serves 4 to 6
Preparation time: **5 mins**
Cooking time: **15 mins**

Japanese Garlic Ginger Steak

4 steak (about 8 oz or 250 g each), excess fat
  trimmed
2 cloves garlic, finely diced
4 tablespoons soy sauce
2 tablespoons *mirin*
1 tablespoon sugar
4 tablespoons rice vinegar
6 oz (175 g) daikon, peeled and thinly sliced
$^1/_2$ carrot, peeled and thinly sliced
1 in (2$^1/_2$ cm) fresh ginger, thinly sliced
1 tablespoon oil
2 spring onions, thinly sliced

1 Place the meat in a large baking dish. Combine the
garlic, soy sauce and *mirin* in a small bowl and pour
it over the steak. Marinate for 30 minutes, turning
occasionally.
2 In a small bowl, dissolve the sugar in the vinegar.
Arrange the daikon, carrot and ginger in a large bowl
and pour the vinegar over it. Set aside for 5 to 10
minutes. Drain and squeeze out any excess moisture
from the vegetables.
3 Heat the oil in a large skillet over high heat. Add the
steak and cook until done to taste. For medium rare,
cook for about 3 minutes on each side.
4 Remove the steak and place it on warmed individual serving plates. Sprinkle with the spring onions
and serve with the marinated vegetables.

Serves 4
Preparation time: **30 mins**
Cooking time: **10 mins**

Stir-fried Pork with Ginger and Cabbage

3 tablespoons soy sauce
2 tablespoons fresh
  ginger juice
2 tablespoons sake
1 teaspoon sugar
2 tablespoons oil
1 lb (450 g) pork tender-
  loin, thinly sliced
³/₄ cup (120 g) Chinese
  or Napa cabbage, cut
  into small squares
2 in (5 cm) fresh ginger,
  thinly sliced

Serves 4
Preparation time: **10 mins**
Cooking time: **6 mins**

1 To make the sauce, combine the soy sauce, ginger juice, sake and sugar in a small bowl. Stir until the sugar is dissolved.

2 Heat 1 tablespoon of the oil in a large skillet over high heat. Stir-fry the pork until the meat is partially cooked, about 1 minute. Remove the pork from the skillet and drain.

3 Add the remaining oil to the skillet. Stir-fry the cabbage and ginger until almost tender, about 2 minutes. Return the pork to the skillet and add the sauce mixture. Stir-fry over high heat until the pork is cooked through, about 2 minutes. Serve with rice.

Sliced Beef in Ginger Soy Gravy

4 medium potatoes, peeled and cut into chunks
1 lb (450 g) sirloin steak
1 medium onion, peeled
2 tablespoons oil
2 cups (500 ml) Basic Dashi Stock (page 16) or 1 teaspoon instant *dashi* granules dissolved in 2 cups (500 ml) boiling water
3 tablespoons sake
2 tablespoons sugar
3 tablespoons soy sauce
2 in (5 cm) fresh ginger, thinly sliced

Serves 4
Preparation time: **35 mins**
Cooking time: **20 mins**

1 Place the potato chunks in a bowl of cold water.
2 Freeze the steak for 30 minutes to firm. Cut across the grain into very thin slices.
3 Halve the onion lengthwise, and slice each half.
4 Heat 1 tablespoon of the oil in a saucepan over medium to high heat. Add the beef and stir-fry until the meat is just brown, about 2 minutes. Remove from the pan and drain.
5 Heat the remaining oil in the pan over medium to high heat. Add the onion and potatoes and stir-fry for 2 minutes until the potatoes are coated with the oil.
6 Add the *dashi* stock, sake and sugar, and bring to a boil over medium heat. Just before it boils, reduce the heat and add the soy sauce and beef. Simmer until the potatoes are tender, about 15 minutes.
7 Garnish with the ginger and serve immediately.

Sukiyaki (Sweet Soy Beef and Vegetable Hotpot)

12 dried or fresh shiitake mushrooms, stems discarded
1 lb (450 g) beef tenderloin, thinly sliced
8 oz (250 g) dried *shirataki* or glass noodles
8 oz (250 g) firm tofu, cubed
2 small leeks, rinsed and sliced diagonally
4 oz (125 g) spinach, washed and coarsely sliced
2 tablespoons oil
4 large eggs or Ponzu Sauce (page 15)

Sauce
3/4 cup (175 ml) soy sauce
1/4 cup (60 ml) sake
1/4 cup (60 ml) *mirin*
1/2 cup (125 ml) water

1 If using dried mushrooms, soak in hot water for 20 minutes until soft. Drain the mushrooms and squeeze out any excess moisture.

2 Combine the Sauce ingredients in a bowl and set aside.

3 Arrange the mushrooms, beef, *shirataki* noodles, tofu and spinach in 4 batches.

4 Heat the oil in a hotpot on a tabletop hotplate. Stir-fry the ingredients in batches until the food is cooked to taste. Cook the rest of the food in similar batches.

5 Diners can use chopsticks to take the cooked meat or vegetables from the hotpot. Use the eggs as a dipping sauce. If you are concerned that the raw eggs may contain salmonella, use the Ponzu Sauce instead.

6 Replenish the hotpot with the remaining ingredients as needed.

Serves 4
Preparation time: **20 mins**
Cooking time: **20 mins**

Shabu-Shabu (Sliced Beef Hotpot)

Sesame Seed Sauce (page 14)

3 spring onions, thinly sliced

Ponzu Sauce (page 15)

1/2 cup daikon, grated

4-in piece *konbu*, wiped and cut in 4 strips

6 cups water

8 oz (250 g) dried *shirataki* or glass noodles

1 lb (450 g) beef tenderloin, thinly sliced

10 oz (300 g) firm tofu, cubed

8 fresh shiitake mushrooms, stems discarded

4 leaves Chinese or Napa cabbage

4 oz (125 g) spinach leaves, rinsed and stalks discarded

2 small leeks, rinsed and thinly sliced diagonally

1/2 teaspoon salt

2 cups cooked udon noodles (optional)

1 Pour the Sesame Seed Sauce into a small bowl and garnish with the spring onions. Set aside.

2 Pour the Ponzu Sauce into a small bowl and garnish with the daikon. Set aside.

3 Blanch the *shirataki* noodles for 1 minute, drain and cut into 4-in (10-cm) lengths.

4 Put the *konbu* and water into a stockpot and bring to a boil over medium heat. Just before it boils, remove the *konbu*. Set the stock aside.

5 Arrange ingredients in 4 batches—vegetables, *shirataki* noodles and tofu—into a hotpot on a table-top hotplate. Ladle enough stock over the ingredients to cover it, and simmer.

6 Diners can cook their meat by holding a slice of the beef with chopsticks or a fondue fork and swishing it in the simmering stock for 10 to 20 seconds, dipping the cooked beef in the sauce of choice and seasoning with salt, as desired. As the other ingredients cook, diners can help themselves from the hotpot.

7 Replenish the hotpot with the remaining ingredients as required, and ladle in more of the stock as it boils down. Continue until all the food is cooked.

8 When all the ingredients are used up, pour the remaining stock, if any, into the hotpot. Cook the udon noodles in the simmering broth for 3 minutes. Ladle the noodles into individual serving bowls and serve.

Serves 4
Preparation time: **30 mins**
Cooking time: **20 mins**

Japanese Sponge Cake (Kasutera)

5 large eggs
$^2/_3$ cup (150 g) caster or superfine sugar
$^1/_4$ cup (60 ml) honey
$^3/_4$ teaspoon baking powder
$^3/_4$ cup (90 g) all-purpose flour
Additional caster sugar for dusting

Serves 6 to 8
Preparation time: **10 mins**
Cooking time: **30 mins**

1 Preheat oven to 350°F (180°C/Gas mark 4). Grease and flour a 9-in (22$^1/_2$-cm)-square baking pan.
2 Break the eggs into a bowl and beat until frothy. Beat in the sugar and honey gradually. Continue beating until the mixture is thick and pale and the eggbeater leaves a thin ribbon, about 12 minutes.
3 Sift the baking powder and flour together into the bowl with the egg mixture.
4 Gently fold the dry ingredients into the egg mixture until just combined. Carefully pour the mixture into the prepared cake pan.
5 Bake for 30 minutes. Remove from the heat and cool completely on a wire rack.
6 Dust with caster sugar and cut into squares before serving.

Beat the egg mixture for about 12 minutes until it leaves a ribbon trail.

Cool the cake on a wire rack and dust with caster sugar.

Green Tea Ice Cream

1 pint (600 ml) vanilla
ice cream
1 tablespoon green tea
powder (*matcha*, page 6)
One 13-oz (400 g) can of
sweetened red beans
(*azuki*, see page 7)
(optional)

1 Blend the ice cream and green tea powder
together, and freeze in a plastic container. For an
interesting variation, serve the Green Tea Ice Cream
with the sweetened red beans.

Serves 4
Preparation time: **5 mins**

Peach Jelly (Momo No Kanten)

4-5 long strips of agar-agar (page 5)
2 cups (500 ml) water
1$^1/_2$ cups (330 g) sugar
$^1/_2$ cup fresh white peaches (from 2 small peaches), cubed
Juice from $^1/_2$ lemon
2 eggs (egg whites only)

Serves 4
Preparation time: **50 mins**
Cooking time: **20 mins**

1 Rinse the agar-agar in cold water, place it in a saucepan and cover with water. Set aside to soak for 20 to 30 minutes.
2 Bring the agar-agar and water to a boil, cooking until the agar-agar is dissolved. Add the sugar and stir until completely dissolved.
3 Drizzle the lemon juice on the peach cubes and set aside.
4 Beat the egg whites into a meringue, then fold in the peach mixture.
5 Pour the jelly mixture into a shallow dish and chill in the refrigerator until set. Serve chilled.

Complete Recipe Listing